AF904093

What It's Worth:
Value and Business Challenges in the Budding Cannabis Industry

A BVR SPECIAL REPORT

BVR
What It's Worth
1000 SW Broadway, Suite 1200, Portland, OR 97205
503-291-7963 • www.bvresources.com

BVR
What It's Worth

Editor: Janice Prescott

Publisher: Sarah Andersen

Managing Editor/Desktop Editor: Monique Nijhout-Rowe

Senior Copy Editor: David Solomon

Chair and CEO: David Foster

President: Lucretia Lyons

Vice President of Sales: Lexie Gross

Customer Service Manager: Retta Dodge

ISBN: 978-1-62150-074-2

Library of Congress Control Number: 2016952663

Table of Contents

Introduction

The times they are a-changin'.
—Bob Dylan

The estimated annual demand for recreational cannabis now exceeds that for wine, craft beer, and organic food,[1] according to estimates gathered for the *Marijuana Business Factbook 2016*. The vast majority of this $40 billion to $45 billion is spent on the black market and so is not taxed.

In the past year, Oregon, Alaska, and Washington, D.C., joined Colorado and the state of Washington in legalizing recreational marijuana. As of the fall of 2016, 25 U.S. states, the District of Columbia, and the territory of Guam allow for comprehensive public medical marijuana and cannabis programs. An additional 17 states allow "low THC" products for medical reasons in limited situations.[2]

Legal marijuana has become serious business. ArcView Market Research estimates that sales of legal marijuana in 2016 will grow to $7.1 billion, an increase of 26% over 2015's $5.7 billion and $4.6 billion the year before.[3] One analyst, GreenWave Advisors, predicts that, in a scenario in which the momentum toward legality included all states by 2020, U.S. retail marijuana sales could reach $35 billion.[4] Alternatively, even if the progression were slower paced, GreenWave expects it to be a $25 billion industry by 2020.

California, the largest state market and the first to legalize medical marijuana, in 1996, accounted for 49% of U.S. cannabis sales in 2014. That amount will grow exponentially if voters legalize adult

1 Marijuana Business Daily, *Marijuana Business Factbook 2016*, Executive Summary.
2 National Conference of State Legislatures, blog, July 7, 2016. www.ncsl.org/research/health/state-medical-marijuana-laws.aspx.
3 ArcView Market Research, *The State of the Legal Marijuana Markets, 4th* edition, Executive Summary, 2016. www.arcviewmarketresearch.com.
4 GreenWave Advisors, *State of the Emerging Marijuana Industry, Current Trends and Projections*, 2nd edition, Executive Summary, November 2015.

use of marijuana in November 2016. Legal marijuana in Colorado, the first state to allow both adult use (also referred to as "recreational") and medical marijuana, was a $996 million industry in 2015, generating $135 million in tax revenue, licenses, and fees. Big players are emerging, who have warehouses with some 50,000 to 60,000 square feet of plants and 50 employees or more watering the plants and giving them nutrients. These are very much commercial, professionally run operations.

And, as with other businesses, there is real money to fight over when the owners divorce a spouse, dispute a partnership agreement, gift shares, or sell the enterprise. However, in this case, performing an accurate valuation is particularly challenging. The industry's relatively short history, high level of risk, high volatility, and complex, quickly evolving regulatory structure are unique considerations to which appraisers, business owners, and attorneys must pay attention. Determining the subject company's proper risk-adjusted discount rate or the valuation multiple to apply to cash flow and EBITDA can be especially problematic. And the ethical or legal issues must be considered since selling marijuana is still considered an illegal activity at the federal level.

Accountants, business appraisers, attorneys, and investors are all paying attention to this booming industry because of the opportunities it provides. The chapters here in *What It's Worth: Value and Business Challenges in the Budding Cannabis Industry* address the important issues and provide the technical insight that business professionals need when valuing or servicing a marijuana dispensary.

Ronald L. Seigneur, CPA/ABV, ASA, CVA, CFF, CGMA
Seigneur Gustafson LLP

1. The Unique Challenges for Business Valuation in the Cannabis Industry

Business valuation experts are hired to quantify risk. The No. 1 challenge the cannabis industry faces is that it is *illegal* under federal law to grow or sell the product the industry is built around. The overwhelming majority of risks—aside from the usual weather problems with agricultural products—essentially stem from that circumstance or variations on it.

Twenty-five U.S. states and the District of Columbia now have made medical marijuana, and thus dispensaries, legal. Four states plus Washington, D.C., and the territory of Guam have legalized marijuana for recreational/adult use. Some 17 states have voted down legalized medical marijuana in the past year, indicating continued ferment around the issue. The cannabis industry is said to be the fastest growing in the country. However, the U.S. government classifies the plant as a Schedule I narcotic, along with heroin and LSD, under the Controlled Substances Act (CSA),[1] which means it has no currently acceptable medical value.

Who ya gonna call? Though the federal government says it is illegal to grow or sell marijuana, it is not illegal according to the states that have legalized it, and in fact the industry is thriving. However, under the CSA, those who advise and assist clients in the cannabis industry can technically be found to be aiding and abetting under the applicable federal statutes. That leaves the professionals who provide legal and accounting services to the trade walking a very fine line, to say the least! The professional associations have strong codes of ethics against providing services to illegal businesses, but those who think time is on the side of legality insist that lawyers and accountants are going to be an important part of sorting out the issues, including those that will arise once (or if)

1 The Controlled Substances Act (CSA) is the statute establishing federal U.S. drug policy under which the manufacture, importation, possession, use, and distribution of certain substances is regulated. It was passed by the 91st United States Congress as Title II of the Comprehensive Drug Abuse Prevention and Control Act of 1970 and signed into law by President Richard Nixon.

it is unquestionably declared legal, as many expect. Accountant Jim Marty is at the center of the swirl of issues that surround the providing of services to marijuana businesses. In Chapter 2, he delves into the ethical questions encountered and describes the attempts at a solution.

Though it was once unthinkable that cannabis would be legalized in any manner, many are now in agreement that change is indeed on the march. Some in the business think the feds just want to wait it out until the dust settles—that they aren't looking for trouble with those who keep their noses clean and operate according to legitimate business practice. Others aren't so sure. Jim Marty and business appraiser Ron Seigneur wrestle with these issues and others as they discuss how to put a value on a marijuana dispensary in Chapters 3 and 4.

The cash economy. A major difficulty for the industry is that banks are often unwilling to set up accounts or accept checks because they fear being caught up in a federal crackdown. Landlords shy away from tenants that might be closed down in a police raid or have their property seized.

Without banking services, companies must make all of their transactions in cash, an activity that brings its own set of problems. So the business has to pay employees, suppliers, and landlords—as well as taxes—in cash, in an economy that hardly uses it.

However, this is changing, as about a dozen banks in Colorado are now providing checking accounts for cannabis businesses across the state. At the time of this writing, it is estimated that about half the marijuana businesses in Colorado have checking accounts. These accounts are expensive, with fees of around $3,000 a month. The banks also require vigorous compliance and oversight, such as providing monthly sales figures and financial statements.

The bank problem is far from solved in many other states, including Nevada, where currently no banks are offering accounts to operators in the cannabis industry.

And, yes, taxes. Just because it is illegal doesn't mean a business doesn't owe taxes. Cannabis growers and retailers pay a very high effective tax rate because the Internal Revenue Code (IRC) §280E limits normal business deductions if a business "consists of trafficking in controlled substances." In a point/counterpoint attempt at a solution, one strategy has been to move overhead up into cost of goods sold (COGS) and ending inventory, using another section, IRC §263A and the regulations under IRC §471, as the basis. But, like everything in this murky field, whether this solution will ultimately pass muster is not clear.

Federal clarifications. Since October 2009, the Departments of Justice (DOJ) and Treasury and the Internal Revenue Service have issued a series of clarifications that often lent themselves to dueling interpretations, sometimes seeming to raise more questions than they resolved.

The most recent memo, released in January 2015 by the office of the chief counsel of the IRS (CCM), takes up the question of determining the COGS in light of IRC §280E when the taxpayer is "trafficking" in a controlled substance. Issued as part of an internal discussion, it casts a disapproving eye on one of the few options for a cannabis business attempting to capitalize its costs. The CCM makes it clear that the IRS will continue to deny deductions for what it considers "selling costs" such as retail rent, retail labor, and advertising.

In Chapter 5, Andrew DeWeese and Calvin Eib, lawyers with the Oregon Cannabis Law Group, explain the significance of this discussion in more detail.

Two legal cases continue to serve as guidance for those working to determine what rules to follow in interpreting IRC §280E. Tony Nitti, CPA and tax partner at WithumSmith+Brown, explains the differences between the 10th Circuit's decision in *CHAMP* and the 9th Circuit's decision in *Olive* in Chapter 6, originally published by Forbes. Court opinions for the two cases are available for download at www.bvresources.com/cannabisolive and www.bvresources.com/cannabischamp.

Memos from the DOJ have tended to focus on enforcement of the Controlled Substances Act. The October 2009 memorandum (widely known as the Ogden memo), was issued by David Ogden, deputy attorney general, after a few states had begun to legalize medical marijuana. It indicated that, while "prosecution of significant traffickers of illegal drugs, including marijuana," remained a core priority, it was likely not an efficient use of federal resources to focus enforcement efforts on individuals with cancer or other serious illnesses who use marijuana as part of a recommended treatment regimen consistent with applicable state law—or on their caregivers.

The first Cole memorandum, issued by James Cole, deputy attorney general, in June 2011 (often referred to as the Cole I memo), reiterated that the DOJ is committed to the enforcement of the Controlled Substances Act, even in states where cannabis is legally grown and distributed, particularly in regard to "federal money laundering statutes and other federal financial laws."

Two years later, the second Cole memorandum (Cole II memo), on Aug. 29, 2013, responding to the fact that so many states had legalized marijuana for medicinal, agricultural, or recreational use, spelled out eight priorities for marijuana enforcement given the department's limited investigative and prosecutorial resources:

- Preventing the distribution of marijuana to minors;
- Preventing revenue from the sale of marijuana from going to criminal enterprises, gangs, and cartels;
- Preventing the diversion of marijuana from states where it is legal under state law in some form to other states;
- Preventing state-authorized marijuana activity from being used as cover or pretext for the trafficking of other illegal drugs or illegal activity;
- Preventing violence and the use of firearms in the cultivation and distribution of marijuana;
- Preventing drugged driving and the exacerbation of other adverse public health consequences associated with marijuana use;

- Preventing the growing of marijuana on public lands and the attendant public safety and environmental dangers posed by marijuana production on public lands; and
- Preventing marijuana possession or use on federal property.

The memorandum adds that "nothing herein precludes investigation or prosecution, even in the absence of any one of the factors, ... in particular circumstances where the investigation and prosecution otherwise serve an important federal interest."

Nobody wants a cash economy with its attendant ills of money laundering, guns, and armed conflict. Since the industry is legal on the state levels and clearly doing business, the U.S. government has an interest in encouraging the banks to be involved, according to James Cole, now former deputy attorney general, in an interview with *Marijuana Business Daily*.[2] Cole issued a third memorandum in February 2014 to clarify the need to prevent financial crimes in relation to marijuana sales.

The U.S. Treasury also took up the problem of banking in February 2014 in the "FinCEN memo," in which the Financial Crimes Enforcement Network aimed to clarify the requirements of the Bank Secrecy Act (BSA). Arriving soon after the Cole II memo, it too attempts to address the conundrum of businesses caught between legal and illegal jurisdictions and assist the industry in its need for banking services. As analyzed by Payment Law Advisor,[3] it lays out "due diligence and risk assessment mandates" for financial institutions providing services to the marijuana industry. These include the priorities of the Cole memo, among others. But it does not relieve the financial organizations of their obligation to file suspicious activity reports (SARs) on the cannabis-related businesses and, in fact, created three new categories uniquely for these businesses.

Thus financial institutions remain reluctant to get involved in what is undoubtedly still a sticky wicket of an industry. Those who do offer services are reluctant to discuss it or to take on new customers. They are watchful for new developments ... but wary in the meantime.

Other challenges for professionals working in the industry. What financial records do you keep when you are working with a legal/illegal business that deals exclusively in cash but pays taxes on the proceeds? How do you set up the business? And how does that differ from the books and records you are familiar with in other industries? In Chapter 7, Jim Marty discusses the unique aspects of a marijuana dispensary's financial records.

In Chapter 8, Hilary Bricken, lead attorney with the Canna Law Group, answers questions about the value drivers of the marijuana industry. Chapter 9 discusses the role of investors in legal marijuana, featuring an interview with Troy Dayton, CEO of the ArcView Investor Network.

It can be difficult to get financial information when valuing medical marijuana dispensaries. In Chapter 10, we present key financial data, including financial statements and financial ratios, to

2 "The Famous Marijuana Memos: Q&A With Former DOJ Deputy Attorney General James Cole," July 27, 2016. mjbizdaily.com/the-famous-marijuana-memos-qa-with-former-doj-deputy-attorney-general-james-cole/.

3 Karen Ross, "Marijuana, Banking, and the '10-Foot Pole,'" April 28, 2014. www.paymentlawadvisor.com/2014/04/28/marijuana-banking-and-the-10-foot-pole/.

help you benchmark a dispensary's performance. This information, going back to 2013, comes from the *BizMiner Industry Financial Report*.

Finally, for further information, the selected bibliography provides you with articles, websites, regulatory information, and market and industry research reports.

What next? Though federal law now considers the growing and selling of marijuana to be illegal, many expect the federal law to change, and GreenWave Advisors is among them:

> The federal government's "allow for now" policies suggest that it is warming up to the idea of full legalization. Also, lawmakers on both sides of the aisle continue to push various pieces of legislation to ease current laws. What is driving this is that the medical benefits of marijuana are becoming better understood, and that politicians are becoming more mindful of the positive economic impact of legalization. Perhaps most important, public support in favor of legalization is growing.[4]

Those servicing marijuana businesses—accountants, appraisers, and attorneys, for starters—certainly have their work cut out for them. These experts who are tackling the challenges of one of the fastest-growing industries in the country need to stay tuned for continuing developments and be ready to respond to changes as they happen.

4 GreenWave Advisors, *State of the Emerging Marijuana Industry, Current Trends and Projections*, Executive Summary, November 2015.

2. Professional Ethics for Those Servicing the (Illegal) Marijuana Industry

Editor's note: Growing and selling marijuana are illegal on the federal level until and unless the U.S. Congress says otherwise. Yet many states have legalized it for both medical and adult/recreational use. The professionals who provide accounting, valuation, and legal services, among others, are bound by the ethical principles of their specialty. Is there wiggle room for those who want to help sort out the issues and solve the problems in what many believe will be a fully legal industry sooner rather than later? Jim Marty, CPA/ABV, MS, believes professionals play a vital role in keeping these businesses on the right side of the law.

Marty polled audience members in his session at an October 2015 AICPA business valuation conference about their willingness to work for a marijuana business. Here are the questions and the results:

> *Would your firm accept a marijuana business client for tax and accounting work?*
>
> *Yes: 45%*
> *No: 55%*
>
> *Would your firm accept a marijuana business for a valuation engagement?*
>
> *Yes: 61%*
> *No: 39%*

In a May 2016 talk to the AIPCA divorce conference in New Orleans, Marty asked the same questions, and the results were nearly unanimous in favor of both. So, yes, the times they are a changing and very quickly.

In this update of a BVR webinar, Marty, who is managing partner of Bridge West CPAs and Consultants, discusses the ethical issues that arise when providing accounting and valuation services to a marijuana dispensary and the different tacks taken in different jurisdictions.

* * *

After Deputy Attorney General David Ogden issued the memorandum regarding the "Investigations and Prosecutions in States Authorizing the Medical Use of Marijuana"[1] in 2009, Colorado lawyers and CPAs with medical marijuana dispensary clients were in uncharted territory. They weren't even sure what questions to ask. Today, they at least know what the questions are, but we are still working on the answers.

Marijuana is still a Schedule I controlled substance, right up there with heroin and cocaine on the federal drug schedules. IRC §280E states:[2]

> No deduction or credit shall be allowed for any amount paid or incurred during the taxable year in carrying on any trade or business if such trade or business (or the activities which comprise such trade or business) consists of *trafficking* in controlled substances (within the meaning of schedule I and II of the Controlled Substances Act) which is prohibited by Federal law or the law of any State in which such trade or business is conducted.

That means retail rent, advertising, retail labor, professional fees, telephone—anything related to the retail dispensary—are not deductible.

The IRS is vigorously enforcing IRC §280E, as discussed in Chapter 5 by Andrew DeWeese and Calvin Eib of the Oregon Cannabis Law Group. Our first Tax Court case for a Colorado dispensary, *Feinberg v. Commissioner,* is still wending its way through the legal system. The question we are asking the courts is: "If you have a license from the state of Colorado hanging on your wall, are you really trafficking in illegal drugs or are you really an agent of the state?"

Other big questions are: "What is the definition of 'trafficking' as put forward in 280E? Does the IRS have the power to assume marijuana businesses are guilty of a crime when they have never been charged or convicted of such crime?

Furthermore, what about the lack of banking services? Legal marijuana is the fastest-growing industry in the country. According to ArcView Group, the U.S. market for legal cannabis grew 232% in 2015, to $5.7 billion, up from $4.6 billion in 2014. Colorado alone had combined medical and recreational sales of just under $1 billion in 2015. ArcView projects U.S. sales of $7.1 billion in 2016. However, this is an industry without one dime of conventional bank financing available. The few banks willing to work with these businesses tend to be locally owned. Much of the business has been self-financed through friends and family, as shown in the exhibit. The auditors and regulators have a new box on their checklist: Do you service medical marijuana clients? As for the banks, when they answer "yes" to this question, the regulators, in the past, have asked them to close the accounts of marijuana businesses.

As noted in Chapter 1, as of August 2016, about a dozen banks in Colorado are openly offering

1 For access to this and other regulatory statements, see the bibliography at the end of this report. www.justice.gov/sites/default/files/opa/legacy/2009/10/19/medical-marijuana.pdf.

2 26 U.S. Code § 280E - Expenditures in connection with the illegal sale of drugs. Legal Information Institute. Cornell University Law School. www.law.cornell.edu/uscode/text/26/280E.

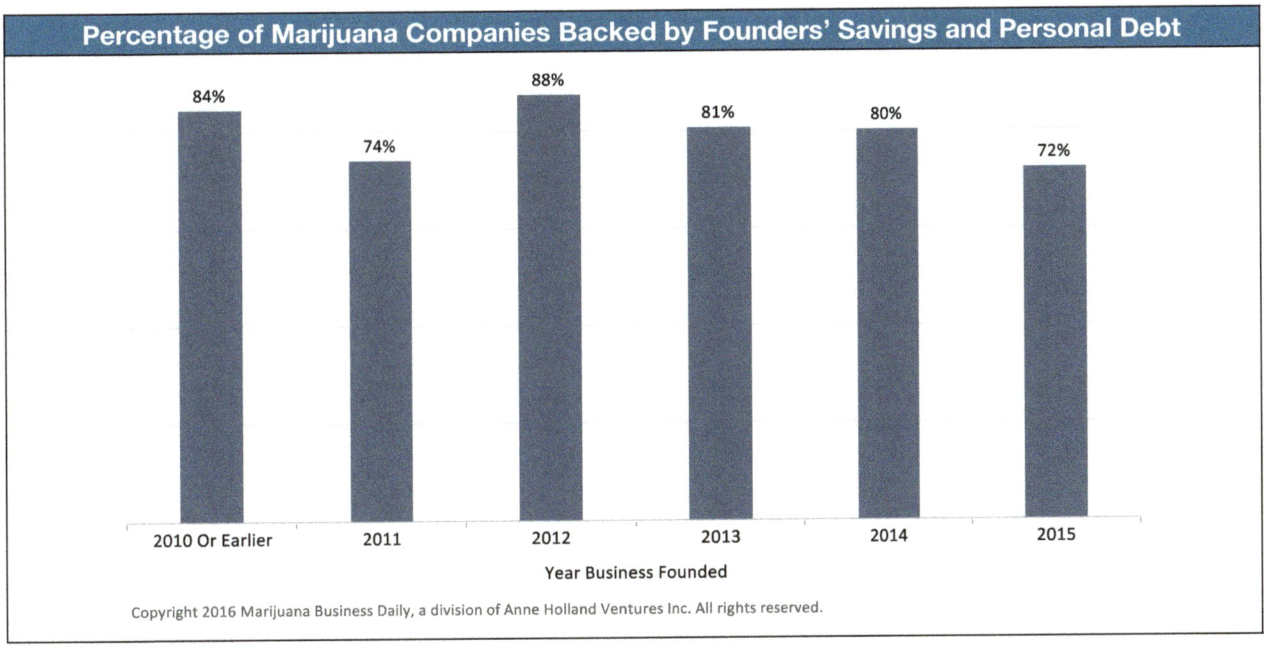

checking accounts to cannabis businesses, but, in other states, such as Nevada, currently no banks are offering cannabis accounts. It appears this problem is on its way to being solved, but there is still a long way to go.

The recently passed Ohio medical marijuana legislation has a provision asking state-chartered banks and credit unions to service the industry there.

Here are the major unresolved questions for CPAs and lawyers working in the marijuana industry:

- Can CPAs, lawyers, and other professional advisers work in the marijuana industry without crossing ethical or legal lines?
- Do IRC sections 280E and 263A apply to the industry?
- How can the industry function without banking services?

These issues were not totally resolved in the restated position of the Department of Justice in the 2011 memorandum from Deputy Attorney General James Cole titled "Guidance Regarding the Ogden Memo in Jurisdictions Seeking to Authorize Marijuana for Medical Use." This memo states: "Persons who are in the business of cultivating, selling or distributing marijuana, and those who knowingly facilitate such activities, are in violation of the Controlled Substances Act, regardless of state law."[3]

The American Bar Association's (ABA) Model Rule of Professional Conduct 1.2(d) dictates that "a lawyer shall not counsel a client to engage, or assist a client, in conduct that the lawyer knows is criminal or fraudulent."[4] Other states have taken different tacks.

3 http://1.usa.gov/1v971f0.
4 http://bit.ly/1mPg29S.

In Maine, it is understood that the federal law is not being enforced right now, but the federal law might ultimately be enforced to the misfortune of lawyers or accountants who have enabled these dispensaries to operate. The state may well be in the vanguard regarding the medical use and effectiveness of marijuana. However, rule 1.2(d), which governs attorney conduct, does not make a distinction between crimes that are enforced and those that are not.

Arizona has taken another approach. The State Bar of Arizona states:[5]

> A lawyer may ethically counsel or assist a client in legal matters expressly permissible under the Arizona Medical Marijuana Act ("Act"), despite the fact that such conduct potentially may violate applicable federal law. Lawyers may do so only if: (1) at the time the advice or assistance is provided, no court decisions have held that the provisions of the Act relating to the client's proposed course of conduct are preempted, void or otherwise invalid; (2) the lawyer reasonably concludes that the client's activities or proposed activities comply fully with state law requirements; and (3) the lawyer advises the client regarding possible federal law implications of the proposed conduct if the lawyer is qualified to do so, or recommends that the client seek other legal counsel regarding those issues and appropriately limits the scope of the representation.

In March 2014, the Colorado Supreme Court approved a rule change that eliminates the threat of ethics sanctions of lawyers in the state that work with marijuana businesses. The updated rule states:[6]

> A lawyer may ... assist a client in conduct that the lawyer reasonably believes is permitted by these constitutional provisions and the statutes, regulations, orders, and other state and local provisions implementing them.

What are the implications? Until recently, no state boards of accounting had taken the type of positions that the bar associations did. However, in late 2015, the Colorado State Board of Accounting passed a provision stating that Colorado CPAs who work with marijuana clients will not be considered to violate their professional ethics. In the meantime, state and local governments across Colorado and other states are rolling out very complex regulations and taxes. Colorado voters approved an excise tax at the wholesale level to tax marijuana in a way similar to the liquor industry.

It is a situation in which the local municipalities and states need the CPAs and lawyers involved. In states where there is some type of legal marijuana, state accountancy boards should give direction to CPA license holders about working in this industry, as has been done in Colorado and Washington state.

Who is a CPA's public? Remember, the middle initial in "CPA" stands for "public"—certified *public* accountant. The "public" stands for the public interest. We are to act with integrity and not be subordinated to personal gain or damage. We are to be objective and independent and free of conflicts of interest when we discharge our professional responsibilities.

5 http://bit.ly/1wvHOz1.
6 http://bit.ly/1vFalhC.

According to AICPA ET Section 53—Article II The Public Interest:[7]

> Members should accept the obligation to act in a way that will serve the public interest, honor the public trust, and demonstrate commitment to professionalism.

When the public votes to make legal an activity such as growing and selling marijuana, it is a public policy. The AICPA anticipated this many years ago, and its ethics rules note that CPAs do have a role in sorting out conflicts, including conflicts between different branches of government. As one of my lawyer friends told me, just because there is a conflict between the federal and state law, lawyers and accountants are not precluded from working in the marijuana industry. In fact, the lawyers and the accountants will eventually help resolve these conflicts.

As long as we act in a professional manner, nothing at the state level prevents CPAs from accepting clients in the marijuana industry. We do, however, have to comply with the AICPA's code of professional conduct. Again, in Colorado, that code of conduct prescribes integrity and not being engaged in fraud, deceit, or any form of dishonesty; it addresses not misrepresenting facts or subordinating judgment to others.

In his article "Federal Income Taxation of Medical Marijuana Businesses," Professor Edward Roche at the University of Denver goes into great detail on IRS Code §263A as it affects this industry. Roche's opinion is that §263A, which relates to moving overhead up into cost of goods sold and ending inventory, should be applied to marijuana growers. He does not feel that practitioners would get into trouble just for signing a tax return.[8]

But let's face it: We don't just sign tax returns. We ask questions. We advise our clients whether they should be an S corporation, a regular corporation, or an LLC. If we get into these areas, could we be charged with aiding and abetting? Professor Roche concludes that this issue is not free of doubt.

Professors Sam Kamin and Eli Wald, from the same university, wrote an article called "Marijuana Lawyers: Outlaws or Crusaders?" In this article, the authors delve into the aiding and abetting and co-conspirator issues—an issue we should worry about as professionals.[9]

Where does all this leave us? Though rare, cases of lawyer prosecution many times involve securities fraud or attorneys working directly for organized crime families. It might be rare because prosecutors respect the client-attorney privilege as well. Kamin and Wald revisit rule 1.2(d) of the ABA Rules of Professional Conduct:

> A lawyer shall not counsel a client to engage, or assist a client, in conduct that the lawyer knows is criminal or fraudulent, but a lawyer may discuss the legal consequences of any proposed course of conduct with a client and may counsel or assist a client to make a good faith effort to determine the validity, scope, meaning or application of the law.

7 Download a PDF of the Code of Professional Conduct here: pub.aicpa.org/codeofconduct/Ethics.aspx. See section 0.300.030.
8 Edward J. Roche, "Federal Income Taxation of Medical Marijuana Businesses," *Tax Lawyer*, Vol. 66, No. 2, 2013. http://bit.ly/1EZNqEy.
9 Sam Kamin and Eli Wald, "Marijuana Lawyers: Outlaws or Crusaders?" *Oregon Law Review*, 2013. http://bit.ly/1u0BGe0.

The authors believe that a strict reading of this rule fails common sense. The rule fails to define the terms "counsel" and "assist," and the meaning of "discuss" is less than clear. The AICPA and the state bar associations have not prevented us from working in the marijuana industry. But, if any of our clients are charged with federal felonies, could we get pulled in because we are their accountants? Judge Learned Hand issued many famous quotes from the bench in a case called *U.S. v. Peoni*. He says that, for aiding and abetting to apply, you must really be associated with the venture. You wish to bring it about or make it succeed.

For co-conspirators, it is not enough that the defendant knowingly associated with others for criminal purposes. It must be shown that the defendant intends to help achieve those criminal goals. Most states follow this course. An example is: If you lend your car to somebody who then robs a bank, it does not necessarily make you part of that crime.

Kamin and Wald also report that the Maine rule confronts the significance of risk to an attorney when a client is committing a federal felony. The Arizona rule is more concerned with access to the law and a lawyer's role and duty to provide services and help clarify the law.

The authors conclude that, in a highly regulated society, first-class citizenship and the ability to act autonomously under the law require access to the law and therefore lawyers. "When a state chooses to regulate a particular conduct, in this case the cultivation and sale of marijuana, access to the law becomes a necessary aspect of implementing that policy," the authors state.

In November 2014, the IRS published its year-end Advisory Council Public Report. It recommended the IRS publish guidance promptly clarifying that tax professionals will not be considered unethical, will not be targeted for audit, and will not be considered in violation of Treasury Circular 230 solely for representing or preparing a return for a business that is illegal under federal law but legal under state law. Thus, the IRS is letting the tax return preparation community know that it wants to help tax professionals in this new industry.

A CPA or lawyer considering whether to accept a client in the marijuana industry must look at the type of work the client is requesting and decide whether the risk of this business is worth the reward.

Jim Marty, *CPA/ABV, MS, managing partner of Bridge West CPAs and Consultants LLC, can be reached at jmarty@jimmarty.com and 303-651-0304.*

3. Valuing a Cannabis-Related Business: Normal as Apple Pie?

Editor's note: Valuing a cannabis-related business would not be much different from valuing any other business except that this business is based on a product that is illegal to grow or sell under current federal law, as explained in Chapter 1. How this challenge is dealt with in states that have legalized it is the nub of this chapter, updated from a Business Valuation Resources (BVR) webinar presented by Jim Marty, CPA/ABV, MS, and Ron Seigneur, CPA/ABV, ASA, CVA, CFF, CGMA. Both Marty and Seigneur are CPAs and valuation practitioners based in Colorado, one of the first states to legalize adult recreational cannabis.

* * *

When valuing a cannabis business, you can often approach the cash flow analysis with the same formula used in many other valuations: Present value of any asset is equal to the cash flow divided by the risk less growth, as shown in Exhibit 1. The critical issue in this industry, though, is the lack of reliable historical cash flow information, which requires the application of a discounted cash flow analysis based on projected performance.

Exhibit 1. Present Value

$$PV = \frac{CF_1}{k - g}$$

Where

CF_1 = cash flow expected in the next period
k = discount rate
g = growth rate (in perpetuity)

As with any business, with a cannabis retail operation or medical dispensary, you have to switch your net income to a cash flow by adding depreciation and taking away capital expenditures. You also have to add (or subtract) your working capital requirements to get to enterprise cash flow and then take away debt service and add loan proceeds. This brings you to cash flow to equity (see Exhibit 2). Nothing changes in the cannabis industry other than to really understand where these numbers come from.

Exhibit 2. Cash Flow Analysis	
Net income after taxes	
Plus	Depreciation
Less	Capital expenditures
Plus/minus	Working capital requirements
Equals	Enterprise cash flow
Less	Debt service
Plus	Loan proceeds
Equals	Cash flow to equity

Given that this business has operated in the open—officially legal first in Colorado—for less than a decade and many businesses have been around for only a few months or years, it is no surprise that there are very few reliable benchmarks in the cannabis industry from the point of view of a business valuation. More information is emerging, but it is anecdotal for the most part and very jurisdictional-specific.

Business appraisers have to come up with workarounds in this situation. Look at what investors expect to receive in the public stock market, add in the additional risk of being invested in this industry, and then apply professional judgment. In a more established industry, an investor might be content with a 20%-to-25% return; in this one—with the regulatory oversight of federal, state, and municipal authorities and leasing, banking, cash, and security issues—the investor might be looking for a 40%-to-50% return.[1]

Other factors to consider include location, competitors, the depth of management, and whether it has good operating procedures and a formalized long-term lease. Is there adequate parking, visibility, and access? As another example of the radical trends in this sector, enterprises involved in the cultivation part of the industry are seeing very dynamic changes as small urban-based grow operations migrate to larger commercial, often rural, facilities, covering many acres and using state-of-the-art technology.

Thus a cannabis business valuation is similar to any other in some ways, but the particular issues in the cannabis business can affect the cash flow. Pay close attention to vetting forecasts, tax affecting the cash flow, the potential liability to the IRS, and other risk factors unique to the industry. It is important to recognize that finding a dispensary operator with reliable projections will be unusual.

1 Chris Walsh, "Appraising a Marijuana Business: Q&A With Valuations Expert Ronald Seigneur," *Marijuana Business Daily*, Sept. 10, 2014, mjbizdaily.com.

Vetting forecasts. When assessing a forecast, in the cultivation sector, for example, make sure you tour the warehouse and the garden; ask what kind of crop the cannabis growers are expecting to have in the next six months and what their annual capacity is. Get a firm understanding of the expertise involved in the grow and how much tenure these individuals have.

An important factor to consider is the number of plants in the ground. There will be three or more cannabis harvests a year because cannabis growers plant in phases. This "perpetual garden" practice ensures plants can be harvested and dried weekly. Get a thorough understanding of the lighting scheme utilized and the philosophy of the lead cultivator toward target plant sizes and varieties produced.

Ask about crop failures. Even the best operations can have a crop failure, so find out how many failures and why. If the crop failures are minimal, the chance of the business being profitable going forward is very much enhanced. Remember, if you grow it, you can sell it, but price points are beginning to moderate in some markets due to increased capacity, better technology, and competitive pressures.

Various parts of the plant can be sold—not just the desirable flowers that dry into what are called the buds, but the leaves can be harvested and sold to the infused products manufacturers. Ask what the lines of revenue are. Ask about the cannabis growers' expansion plans.

Tax affecting the cash flow. Generally, when tax affecting the cash flow, you want to apply a fairly high marginal rate by taxing the gross profit. If the business has not been handling IRC §280E, regarding the deductibility of business expenses, in compliance with how the IRS would like to see it, you may need to book an unrecorded liability for potential IRS audits. If the dispensary has had IRS audits, ask whether they have been resolved. Remember, many dispensaries have only been in operation for a short period, so check for the possible liability of IRS audits. How is §280E handled? If the dispensaries have been ignoring §280E, consider making a valuation adjustment to record potential IRS tax assessments.

Identifying risk factors. When considering risk in a cannabis business, never forget that the federal government considers selling cannabis illegal. You need to understand the Department of Justice (DOJ) memos (explained in Chapter 1 and listed in the regulatory section of the bibliography in the appendix to this report) and the IRS chief counsel's memo, as explained in Chapter 5, and consider how they affect your risk.

These memos certainly appear to reduce risk; the DOJ is saying, "If the dispensary owner stays compliant, you are actually doing what we want you to do." In fact, the Cole memo basically quotes the Colorado regulatory system, and the guidance it provides is being practiced in Colorado.

Nevertheless, even if your clients are playing by the rules, the DOJ is watching. If they break any of the rules—if the cannabis is consumed or grown on public lands, if it gets into the hands of kids, if it crosses state lines—then there is an issue. Residents can buy an ounce of cannabis for recreational purposes legally in Colorado; people from out of state can come in and buy a fourth of an ounce. But there is no tracking of sales. On South Broadway in Denver, you could stop at 10 to 12 different facilities and buy a quarter ounce at each to take back home. It is only a matter of time before somebody gets caught at the airport or at the border. The police on the Kansas and Nebraska borders are watching interstates 70 and 80 for eastbound travelers. These rules will continue to evolve. That is the conundrum of trying to value the risk.

You have to know your client. You want to make sure your client is ethical and not coloring outside the lines because you don't want to be involved in that. The vast majority of the people involved in this industry are honorable and want to do the right thing and want to see this industry succeed. On the other hand, the cannabis industry continues to attract some unsavory types, and it is paramount that professionals working in the space always be on the lookout for client types that are not a good fit. If we have an interview with somebody and we don't have a good feeling, we generally don't take that person on as a client. That is true of any industry, but a bit more relevant in this sector.

An internal controls assessment is essential. Controls must be in place to prevent diversion by employees. Even if the owners are unaware of this activity, it could cost them their license.

Cash on hand. How are cash payments handled? Are Form 1099s issued? If it is a retail or wholesale operator, has the business complied with the Form 8300 requirements for large cash deposits? As explained in Chapter 1, this is a cash-based business, so you want to make sure that the proper Form 1099s are being issued and the businesses have proper internal controls over cash and inventory. How are the businesses handling their cash? How is their banking handled? This industry has had many workarounds in relation to banking.

Competitive landscape. Consider the local area in which the cannabis business operates. A county with a large population may have only one location due to zoning restrictions, and a business there may do very well because of the lack of competition. On the other hand, for example, an area in Denver called South Broadway has a concentration of dispensaries, making for a more competitive environment. A dispensary in northern Colorado gets most of its sales from the east because, between there and Kansas (around 300 miles), there are no other dispensaries. Since 2014, it has been legal to sell to out-of-state customers, and we now are seeing cannabis tourism in Colorado.

Key employees. In terms of personnel, the head gardener is very much a key employee. The best chance for success in the business is a very strong gardener working in combination with a good businessman or businesswoman. If the cannabis growers have a gardener with no business sense, this could be a problem. Owners in it just for the money, with no growing skills, are at higher risk, too.

Do the owners have relevant business experience? Is the main gardener an owner? If that gardener quits or is let go, not only will the job be vacant, but also the disgruntled former employee could go in at night and destroy the harvest. Gardeners can be very protective of their genetics. Do any of the owners have lurking personal issues that can jeopardize a cannabis license? If multiple owners, do they all get along and work cohesively?

Leases. Is the lease ironclad? Is there bank financing on the property that could go awry? During your interview with members of management, discuss their lease and their option to renew. How is the building financed? Here is a possible scenario: The rent is paid every month, and the landlord is happy with the tenant. Then the three-year balloon comes up on the mortgage. The landlord goes to the bank to refinance, and the bank representative asks, "Who is your tenant?"

> *Landlord:* It is Joe Cannabis Co.
>
> *Bank representative:* Sorry, we won't refinance unless you kick them out.

That can happen both at the retail and the wholesale level. If the owners of a cannabis business are going to rent, ask their landlord about the debt structure. You want a building that is free and clear or has private financing. Another option, if it is financially feasible, is for the owners to purchase the real estate for the grow and retail, eliminating the real estate problem. Another issue can arise when an operation initially granted a medical license then becomes authorized to sell to the retail adult-use market. Have the lease arrangements contemplated this expansion? Anticipating and planning for such contingencies is the only way to avoid adverse consequences.

The problem of banks. One reason banks are reluctant to be involved in this industry in the current climate is that, with central bank processing, Colorado checks clear outside the state, in places that do not have legal cannabis. If the federal government stepped in and enforced the law differently, a lot of checks could bounce. Thus, banks need to know a cannabis retail or dispensary client is fully compliant with state laws and that there is complete control of the product from the grow facility to the retail and then to the bank. Armed security guards and armored trucks that move the cannabis and cash are a must if the business wants to have access to banking.

It is very difficult for banks to do business with an industry that is making large cash deposits and operating illegally according to federal law and still comply with their own regulations under the Bank Secrecy Act (BSA) and anti-money laundering rules.

As noted in Chapter 1, the Payment Law Advisor provides an excellent analysis[2] of the current risks inherent for financial institutions in providing services to the cannabis industry in the context of the Treasury's February 2014 "FinCEN memo." In that memo, the Financial Crimes Enforcement Network aimed to clarify the requirements of the BSA. In a quest for full transparency, a bill named "The Marijuana Businesses Access to Banking Act" has been introduced in both houses of Congress for a number of years, so far without passage.

If the banking problem were easy to solve, someone would have figured it out by now. There has been a robust cannabis industry in Colorado for seven years, and yet there are only a few banks

2 Karen Ross, "Marijuana, Banking, and the '10-Foot Pole,'" April 28, 2014. www.paymentlawadvisor.com/2014/04/28/marijuana-banking-and-the-10-foot-pole/.

openly accepting cannabis business clients, and they do not accept new applications.

The hardest bills to pay without a checking account are taxes on payroll. You have to do an electronic funds transfer (EFT) to pay federal withholding taxes. Thus a cannabis business needs at least one checking account, perhaps a personal checking account used just for those transactions. The rent and other bills are paid in cash.

One cannabis dispensary owner uses his accounting software to generate checks for his payroll on plain white paper. He tells his employees, "Here is your check, really a voucher, for the last week, $329.66, printed right here out of Peachtree. Oh, and by the way, there is only one place in the world you can cash that check, and that is at the dispensary counter right here." That way, all payroll records are created in his system so that he can generate the W-2s at the end of the year. He uses that system with his vendors as well.

Much of the information presented in this chapter is relevant for assignments focused on the appraisal of intellectual property rights in the cannabis industry. There is a substantial need for IP appraisal in this sector due to the value of certain license rights associated with cultivation, retail, and MIPS licenses, in addition to the IP value of branding for operators who have an established brand involving trademarks, trade dress, graphics, and beyond.

This industry is not yet mature, and it is continually evolving. For the authors, it is fascinating to take on appraisal work in more established markets such as Colorado and Washington state, as compared to work assignments in emerging markets, such as Nevada and Maryland, just as examples. A valuation done a year ago in many industries would still be relevant, but, in the shifting sands of this industry, it is likely not to be. There is not yet much activity in terms of mergers and acquisitions. There is pent-up interest. Some people who would love to be involved are waiting on the sidelines for now.[3]

Jim Marty, *CPA/ABV, MS, of Bridge West LLC, can be reached at jmarty@jimmarty.com and 303-651-0304.*

Ron Seigneur, *CPA/ABV, ASA, CVA, CFF, CGMA, of Seigneur Gustafson LLP CPAs, can be reached at ron.seigneur@cpavalue.com and 303-980-1111.*

3 Chris Walsh, "Appraising a Marijuana Business: Q&A With Valuations Expert Ronald Seigneur," *Marijuana Business Daily*, Sept. 10, 2014, mjbizdaily.com.

4. Questions on Valuation and Marijuana Businesses: Replies From Experts in the Field

The BVR webinar Medical Marijuana Update: Accounting, Ethics & Tax Issues, presented by Jim Marty and Ron Seigneur, elicited several questions from the audience. During the webinar, Jim Marty, CPA/ABV, MS, and Ronald Seigneur, CPA/ABV, ASA, CVA, CFF, CGMA, discussed the opportunities, challenges, and obstacles to the financial and legal professions supporting the sellers and dispensaries of cannabis after its legalization in Colorado and Washington in 2012. Both Marty and Seigneur are CPAs and valuation practitioners in Colorado.

Listed below are some of the questions, with answers.

Q: *What are some of the valuation opportunities? Are sales of businesses mostly due to divorce?*

A: Mergers and acquisitions are happening, and, since full legalization passed in Colorado, the value of the dispensaries has increased considerably. A small dispensary with little or no profit may be worth $1 million or more because it has a retail location that is properly zoned and is licensed by the state of Colorado. Stock sales or asset sales are both allowed in Colorado if the final license has been approved.

There are also ongoing consulting opportunities in this industry. Marijuana businesses consist of several segments, such as grow, extraction, processing, edibles, retailing, testing, and other ancillary businesses, among them selling hats, T-shirts, and pipes. Each of these segments has its own characteristics. There are also poor business practices that can be improved. Even if nothing goes wrong, a lot of these business owners are inexperienced, and they don't know how to run a payroll. Two or three years later, they have wasted the better part of a million dollars, and they don't know why they still are not making money.

People get into trouble in this business for various reasons. The owner's license may be revoked, for example, because poor internal controls have led to diversion of pounds of marijuana by employees. Though possibly due to no fault by the owner, the owner will nevertheless pay the price. Once you get in trouble, you can't have a license. Hence, there are many valuation opportunities when the facility goes up for sale.

Furthermore, there are many ancillary industries to the marijuana industry. Think of the products and services that marijuana dispensaries use: packaging, construction, equipment, and real estate, to name a few.

Q: *Doesn't the IRS make you take a reasonable salary in an S corporation?*

A: S corps aren't the best for this industry because they could be double taxed. You have to take that W-2, and it is not deductible unless the owner is working in the garden. C corps can be a good alternative since, if the IRS makes a substantial tax assessment, it will not flow through to the shareholders.

Q: *How likely are we to encounter requests for a valuation where legal compliance is in the early years, and it is questionable?*

A: In the valuation field, you want to come in behind the regulation. The nice thing about this industry is that you don't have to rush into it. You can let it take hold and let it grow (and then come in behind that growth and establish yourself).

From a marketing perspective, you want to make yourself known to the attorneys who are helping these businesses get their licenses. Find groups such as the National Cannabis Industry Association (NCIA) and go to their meetings and events with your business cards. You will get business.

Q: *What about the maintenance costs of idle land waiting to be planted as part of crop rotation?*

A: Anything having to do with growing the plant is deductible as cost of goods sold. If you had idle land that was waiting to be planted, your cost of holding that land would be part of the cost of goods sold.

Q: *What types of valuation multiples are you using?*

A: One multiple I am currently using is about a 30%-to-45% discount rate. You would apply it to an after-tax cash flow using a fairly high marginal tax rate.

For M&A, one multiple that is emerging is one times garden production at retail. If your garden is capable of growing a thousand pounds a year, and you can sell for $3,000 a pound or more, then your combined retail with your OPC is worth $3 million.

Q: *What is the multiple?*

A: Unfortunately, this is a question we just can't answer. The multiple is going to change dramatically going ahead. There are businesses that are not profitable. There are people paying huge premiums for those. So we have this continuing disconnect just as we do in other industries between market multiples and the income method.

Q: *What about a discount for lack of marketability?*

A: There is no difference with this industry. It is just cash flow and risk like every other valuation we ever do.

However, the residency requirement gives you a huge argument for a high discount for lack of marketability. Your only potential buyers are going to be qualified operators who meet the residency requirement in each venue. There is no limit in Colorado, but, in other states, such as Washington, you can't have more than three sites, so that is an issue, too.

Jim Marty, *CPA/ABV, MS, of Bridge West LLC, can be reached at jmarty@jimmarty.com and 303-651-0304.*

Ron Seigneur, *CPA/ABV, ASA, CVA, CFF, CGMA, of Seigneur Gustafson LLP CPAs, can be reached at ron.seigneur@cpavalue.com and 303-980-1111.*

5. IRC Section 280E After IRS Chief Counsel Memorandum 201504011

By Andrew C. DeWeese, Esq., and Calvin E. Eib, Esq.

Editor's note: As explained in Chapter 1, the problem of calculating taxes is a major one for those in cannabis-related businesses. This chapter provides an insightful analysis by the Oregon Cannabis Law Group of the Jan. 23, 2015, memo from the IRS on the question of how taxes are calculated in marijuana-related businesses. It was previously published in the March 2015 issue of Marijuana Venture.[1]

* * *

On Jan. 23, 2015, the IRS released Office of Chief Counsel Memorandum No. 201504011, providing useful insight into the IRS chief counsel's view of how cannabis businesses are required to calculate taxable income for federal income tax purposes and presenting a clear disapproval of the method many in the cannabis industry are using to capitalize costs as cost of goods sold (COGS).

What is §280E? Although cannabis farming and retail businesses are considered illegal under federal law, the IRS still requires them (along with all other businesses with revenues derived from illegal activities) to pay federal income taxes. Cannabis businesses are subject to a very high effective tax rate because of Internal Revenue Code §280E.

Normally, a business is entitled to calculate its taxable income by deducting any ordinary and necessary business expenses from its gross income. However, §280E provides:

> No deduction or credit shall be allowed for any expenditure paid or incurred in carrying on any trade or business if such trade or business (or the activities which comprise such trade or business)

1 Reprinted with permission from both *Marijuana Venture* and Oregon Cannabis Law Group.

> consists of trafficking in controlled substances (within the meaning of schedule I and II of the Controlled Substances Act) which is prohibited by Federal law or the law of any State in which such trade or business is conducted.

Because cannabis is classified as a Schedule I controlled substance under federal law, §280E means that cannabis businesses, even if legal under state law, cannot make normal business deductions. Nevertheless, cannabis businesses have found some relief from §280E by deducting their cost of goods sold.

What is COGS and why is it important? Federal income taxes are, essentially, based on a simple formula: add up "all income, from whatever source derived" (known as your "gross income") and then subtract all your "ordinary and necessary" businesses expenses, and you've got your "taxable income." Gross income includes "all income from whatever source derived" (§61(a)).

However, in the case of taxpayers who have "gains derived from dealings in property" (such as cannabis growers, retailers, among many others), gross income means something slightly different: gross receipts minus COGS.

Therefore, knowing a business's COGS—and what, in particular, may be treated as a cost of goods sold—is critical to understanding and properly calculating taxable income for any inventory-based business, and especially a cannabis business. COGS is important because, in calculating gross income, those costs are netted against gross receipts. In other words, generally, the higher your COGS, the lower your gross income. The concept of COGS enjoys the support and approval of the U.S. Supreme Court, which has held that congressional power to lay and collect income taxes in the context of a reseller or producer means gross income, not gross receipts.

U.S. Tax Court has described COGS as the expenditures needed "to acquire, construct or extract a physical product which is to be sold; the seller can have no gain until he recovers the economic investment that he has made directly in the actual item sold." As a simple example, if you received $100 for something that took you $40 worth of labor and capital to grow (in other words, COGS), then your gross income is $60.

For cannabis businesses, COGS, and the ability to capitalize its expenditures, represents the sole opportunity to reduce its taxable income by its expenditures. When an inventory-costing regulation applies, the business "capitalizes" the expense, keeps that cost in inventories until the taxable year it sells the associated plant or inventory. At that point, the business includes the expense in COGS, which in turn reduces gross receipts, which in turn reduces taxable income.

Many types of businesses might prefer to deduct an expenditure immediately, in the year a piece of equipment or inventory is purchased, rather than having to capitalize it and have its tax benefit spread over future years. This is not the case for a cannabis business: Because of §280E's prohibition on normal business deductions, it is clearly preferable for a cannabis business to capitalize an expenditure whenever possible, rather than having it treated as a nondeductible ordinary and necessary business expense.

This raises an important question: What are the rules for determining which expenses may be included in a cannabis business's cost of goods sold?

Determining COGS in light of Memorandum 201504011. The Chief Counsel Memorandum released on Jan. 23, 2015, sheds some light on these rules, addressing two "accounting-related" issues concerning cannabis businesses.

First, the memo addressed the question: "How does a taxpayer trafficking in a Schedule I or Schedule II controlled substance determine COGS for the purposes of §280E?" The memo concludes that cannabis businesses are entitled to determine inventoriable costs of goods sold using the applicable regulations "as they existed when §280E was enacted" in 1982 and that such businesses are *not* allowed to use more recent IRS regulations found in §263A (known as the UNICAP rules) that have increased the types of expenditures to be included in COGS.

The 1982 regulations are §471 and are referred to as the "full absorption method." After 1982, the IRS pushed for more expenses to be treated as COGS rather than currently deductible, and those rules are referred to as Uniform Capitalization, or more often the acronym "UNICAP." UNICAP goes beyond the §471 rules to include purchasing, handling, and storage expenses, as well as service costs such as the costs associated with payroll, legal, and personnel functions.

Obviously, the more expenses a cannabis business can include in its COGS, the lower its gross income, and, therefore, its tax burden due to the otherwise limited ability to deduct these same expenses outside of COGS. In other words, because UNICAP greatly expanded the categories of costs that qualify as COGS, it is quite favorable to a cannabis business looking to reduce its tax burden.

Unfortunately, one of the biggest impacts of the Chief Counsel Memorandum is that the IRS will no longer allow cannabis businesses to use UNICAP and, instead, will only allow them to capitalize costs includible in COGS as of the passage of §280E—back in 1982. The memo states:

> When §280E was enacted in 1982, "inventoriable cost" meant a cost that was capitalized to inventories under §471 (as those regulations existed before the enactment of §263A). The specific regulations are §1.471-3(b) in the case of a reseller of property and §§1.471-3(c) and 1.471-11 in the case of a producer of property.

By the memo's reasoning, cannabis retail businesses utilizing the §471 inventory rules would include in its COGS:

1. Invoice price of the cannabis purchased, less trade or other discounts; and
2. Transportation or other necessary charges incurred in acquiring possession of the cannabis.

Similarly, a cannabis grower/producer using the §471 inventory method would include in its COGS:

1. Direct material costs (cannabis seeds or plants);
2. Direct labor costs (e.g., planting, cultivating, harvesting, sorting);

3. Category 1 indirect costs (§1.471-11(c)(2)(i)); and
4. "Possibly" Category 3 indirect costs (§1.471-11(c)(2)(iii)).

Why, according to the IRS memo, must a cannabis business use §471 (as of 1982) and not the UNICAP rules?

1. Section 263A states (in a passage commonly referred to as the "flush" language) that "any cost which (but for this subsection) could not be taken into account in computing taxable income for any taxable year shall not be treated as a cost described in this paragraph." Therefore, §280E and §263A, "when read together," prevent a taxpayer trafficking in a Schedule I or Schedule II controlled substance from obtaining a tax benefit by capitalizing otherwise disallowed deductions.
2. Congress did not repeal or amend §280E when it enacted §263A.
3. "Nothing in the legislative history of §263A suggests that Congress intended to permit a taxpayer to circumvent §280E by treating a disallowed deduction as an inventoriable cost or as any other type of capitalized cost."
4. The legislative history of §263A states that "a cost is subject to capitalization … only to the extent it would otherwise be taken into account in computing taxable income for any taxable year."

Therefore, according to the memo: "If a taxpayer subject to §280E were allowed to capitalize additional §263A costs, §263A would cease being a provision that affects merely timing and would become a provision that transforms nondeductible expenses into capitalizable costs."

The memo also concludes that, in situations where the accounting method used by a cannabis business causes a tax result contrary to the 16th Amendment of the U.S. Constitution, to §61(a)(3), and to the legislative history of §280E, the IRS has broad authority to require the business to change its method of accounting regardless of whether that change results in a positive or negative adjustment.

Conclusion. The cannabis industry—and especially in light of the recent passage of HB 3460 and Measure 91, the Oregon cannabis industry—is looking for clarity regarding its federal income tax obligations, so the IRS memo is timely and educational, if not especially welcome. Remember, however, that the memo is only an internal discussion and does not carry any sort of legal weight. It is not a law, regulation, or court case and may not be used or cited as precedent. The IRS could change its mind or take a contrary position any time it desires. However, the memo likely signals more aggressive audits regarding cannabis businesses that may have used the UNICAP rules.

Sooner or later, the U.S. Tax Court (and, ultimately, the U.S. Supreme Court) will have to answer the following questions: (1) Did Congress intend that cannabis businesses must use a definition of COGS as it existed in 1982? (2) The U.S. Tax Court, in *Franklin* (a case that is cited in the memo), said that §280E "deals only with deductions and credits … and does not disallow exclusions from gross income on account of cost of goods sold" and that §280E would not preclude a taxpayer "from taking account of any cost of goods sold." Does the memo conflict with the U.S. Tax Court's view, or perhaps signal a new view, of the reach of §280E? (3) If the IRS takes the view held in the memo, does it create constitutional issues—might the IRS be viewed as impermissibly trying to limit a cannabis business's ability to capitalize its costs?

These questions, and many more, will be on the minds of every taxpayer in the cannabis industry in the coming years.

Andrew DeWeese, *a partner and founder of the Oregon Cannabis Law Group in Portland, Ore., handles cases in state and federal court and represents and advises cannabis business clients on state law compliance issues and federal tax planning and disputes.*

Calvin Eib, *a partner in the Oregon Cannabis Law Group, is licensed to practice law in Oregon and Illinois. With a Master of Laws degree in taxation from the University of Miami, he has more than 19 years of experience practicing in the areas of state and federal tax matters and business regulation, including representing and advising corporate clients on tax compliance and litigation.*

6. 9th Circuit: Legal Or Not, Marijuana Facility Cannot Deduct Its Expenses

By Tony Nitti, CPA

*Editor's note: In this article published by Forbes on July 10, 2015, Tony Nitti, CPA and tax partner at WithumSmith+Brown, examines two legal opinions—*CHAMP *and* Olive*—that so far appear to set the standard for interpreting the applicability of Section 280E of the Internal Revenue Code.* CHAMP *seemed to offer a loophole based on separating the business between growing marijuana and "trafficking" it, but* Olive *makes it clear the rules must be followed precisely. Many in the field do not consider that the final word has been spoken, but the news thus far does not favor "business as usual" in the realm of taxes. The full court opinion for* Olive *is located at www.bvresources.com/cannabisolive and the full court opinion for* CHAMP *is located at www.bvresources.com/cannabischamp.*[1]

* * *

Legalized medicinal marijuana is yesterday's news; legal *recreational* marijuana is the focus now, as with each passing year, additional states are considering the legalize-and-tax regime first instituted by Colorado and Washington. While state law is becoming more accepting of the idea of free-market marijuana, however, a decades-old provision of the *federal* tax code remains firmly in place, threatening to administer a painful amount of tax on marijuana facilities and serving as a greater barrier to entry into the industry than any outdated notion of moral or ethical impropriety.

The IRS has been wielding a little-known Internal Revenue Code section—Section 280E—to wage war on medicinal and recreational marijuana facilities. Section 280E provides that no deduction—other

1 Reprinted with permission from Forbes. From Forbes, July 10, 2015 © 2015 Forbes. All rights reserved. Used by permission and protected by the Copyright Laws of the United States. The printing, copying, redistribution, or retransmission of this Content without express written permission is prohibited.

than the cost to purchase or grow the marijuana inventory, or cost of goods sold (COGS)—shall be allowed for any amount incurred in a business that consists of "trafficking in controlled substances." And while marijuana may have been legalized in several states for medicinal or recreational purposes, because the drug finds itself on Schedule I of the Controlled Substances Act, the IRS has the ammunition necessary to deny all non-COGS deductions – things like rent, utilities, wages, supplies, etc.—of any facility that buys and sells the drug.

While Section 280E is very clear in requiring denial of all non-COGS expenses of a marijuana facility, in the seminal case on the matter—*Californians Helping to Alleviate Medical Problems (CHAMP)*, 128 T.C. 173, (2002)—the taxpayer actually achieved a partial victory against the IRS. In *CHAMP*, while the Tax Court agreed with the IRS's position that Section 280E was applicable to a medicinal dispensary despite the fact that the facility was legal under state law, the court acknowledged that a marijuana facility can have multiple lines of businesses, only one of which is "trafficking in a controlled substance," and thus Section 280E should be applied only to the one offending line of businesses.

The taxpayers in CHAMP were able to effectively argue that only a portion of their business involved the trafficking of marijuana, with the rest of their business focusing on counseling customers on which type of marijuana would best treat their particular ailment; as a result, they were able to salvage the deductions attributable to the counseling business.

The decision in CHAMP has served as a model for other facilities to emulate. In 2012, another California medicinal shop found itself in front of the Tax Court defending its deductions in the face of the Service's application of Section 280E, and in doing so, attempted to duplicate the "multiple lines of business" argument that was successful in CHAMP.

Tax Court's Decision in *Olive*. In *Olive v. Commissioner*, 139 T.C. 2, (2012), however, the taxpayer wasn't so lucky. The Vapor Room—established as a sole proprietorship by its owner, Martin Olive—was a California facility whose sole source of revenue was its sale of medical marijuana. Patrons went to the Vapor Room to relax and smoke or inhale vaporized marijuana, but that was not *all* they did. The Vapor Room is set up like a community center, with couches, chairs, and tables located throughout the establishment. Games, books, and art supplies are available for patrons' general use. The Vapor Room also offers services such as yoga, movies, and massage therapy. Customers can drink tea or water during their visits, or they can eat snacks including pizza and sandwiches. However, all of these additional amenities *were provided free of charge.*

Upon audit, the IRS hit Olive from all angles, asserting that he: 1) understated the income of the Vapor Room; 2) overstated the cost of goods sold; and 3) was not entitled to any operating expenses under Section 280E. Olive and the IRS split on the first two issues. The Tax Court agreed with the IRS that Olive's shoddy records—in his defense, Olive bragged that the industry "shun[s] formal 'substantiation' in the form of receipts"—did not adequately substantiate his revenue. As a result, the court required Olive to include in income the revenue reflected on one of Olive's ledgers, which was significantly in excess of the amounts reported on his tax returns.

With regard to the cost of goods sold, the Tax Court refused to side with the IRS's assertion that because Olive's records were lacking, he wasn't entitled to any deduction for cost of goods sold. Instead, the court looked to the testimony of industry insiders to determine that, on average, the cost of goods sold of medicinal marijuana facilities were approximately 75.16% of revenue. The court then reduced Olive's COGS to account for the fact that he gave away some of his product for free, reasoning that because he gave it away, it wasn't held for sale and thus couldn't be included in cost of goods sold.

Lastly, the Tax Court agreed with the IRS that the Vapor Room was *not* entitled to deduct any of its operating expense pursuant to Section 280E, refusing to afford Olive the wiggle room it showed the taxpayer in *CHAMP*. Despite Olive's contention that his business was similar to the one in *CHAMP*—equal parts the sale of goods and the provision of additional services—the Tax Court was unconvinced:

> Petitioner asserts that the Vapor Room's overwhelming purpose was to provide caregiving services, that the Vapor Room's expenses are almost entirely related to the caregiving business and that the Vapor Room would continue to operate even if petitioner did not sell medical marijuana. We disagree. We find instead that petitioner had a single business, the dispensing of medical marijuana, and that he provided all of the Vapor Room's services and activities as part of that business. The record establishes that the Vapor Room is not the same type of operation as the medical marijuana dispensary in *CHAMP* that we found to have two businesses.

In reaching its decision, the Tax Court established a precedent that it will hold a medicinal marijuana facility to a strict standard in establishing that it offers multiple lines of business:

> Petitioner essentially reads our Opinion in *CHAMP* to hold that a medical marijuana dispensary that allows its customers to consume medical marijuana on its premises with similarly situated individuals is a caregiver if the dispensary also provides the customers with incidental activities, consultation or advice. Such a reading is wrong. Petitioner also has not established that the Vapor Room's activities or services independent of the dispensing of medical marijuana were extensive. We perceive his claim now that the Vapor Room actually consists of two businesses as simply an after-the-fact attempt to artificially equate the Vapor Room with the medical marijuana dispensary in *CHAMP* so as to avoid the disallowance of all of the Vapor Room's expenses under section 280E. We conclude that section 280E applies to preclude petitioner from deducting any of the Vapor Room's claimed expenses.

9th Circuit's Decision in *Olive*. The 9th Circuit finally got around to deciding Martin Olive's appeal in the Tax Court decision. The subject matter was limited to the application of Section 280E to the Vapor Room; specifically, did the Vapor Room have additional lines of business in addition to selling marijuana, which would escape the denial of deductions required by the statute?

The answer was a resounding no. The 9th Circuit quickly concluded that providing additional services to patrons—the freedom to relax, use a vaporizer, and have a bite to eat—*without charging a fee* did not constitute an additional line of business:

> An analogy may help to illustrate the difference between the Vapor Room and the business at issue in *CHAMP*. Bookstore A sells books. It also supplies some complimentary amenities:

> patrons can sit in comfortable seating areas while considering whether to buy a book; they can drink coffee or tea and eat cookies, all of which the bookstore offers at no charge; they can obtain advice from the staff about new authors, book clubs, community events, and the like; they can bring their children to a weekend story time or an after-school reading circle. The "trade or business" of Bookstore A "consists of" selling books. It's many amenities do not alter that conclusion; presumably, the owner hopes to attract buyers of books by creating an alluring atmosphere. By contrast, Bookstore B sells books but also sells coffee and pastries, which customers can consume in a café-like seating area. Bookstore B has two "trades or businesses," one of which consists of selling books and the other of which "consists of" selling food and beverages.

CHAMP, the court concluded, was Bookstore B. The Vapor Room, on the other hand, was Bookstore A:

> The income-generating activities in which the Vapor Room engaged consisted solely of trafficking in medicinal marijuana which, as noted, is prohibited under federal law. Under Section 280E then, the expenses that Petitioner incurred in the course of operating the Vapor Room cannot be deducted for federal purposes.

What's the lesson? The relevant case history provides the precedent that a recreational or medicinal marijuana facility can have multiple lines of business, with only the business engaged in selling marijuana subject to the harsh disallowance provisions of Section 280E. The taxpayer in *Olive,* however, shows a facility exactly what *not* to do if it wants to successfully argue that more than one business exists. While offering services and products to customers for free is perhaps good business practice and undoubtedly a nice gesture, one cannot argue that it is a separate "line of business," because by forgoing a fee, it is clear that there is no intention to make a profit, which is the primary trait of any true business.

It's a strange dichotomy of authority the marijuana industry finds itself governed by—blessed by state law, but persecuted by the IRS. The industry's only saving grace is that it is so insanely profitable, it appears that it is able to survive a draconian tax regime under which its members are taxed on 100% of their gross profits.

Tony Nitti, *CPA and tax partner at WithumSmith+Brown, is a contributor to Forbes, from which this article was taken.*

7. Best Practices for a Marijuana Business's Books and Records

Editor's note: Once again, a marijuana business is much like any other—except when it isn't. A cannabis dispensary or retail business can be quite lucrative. As an evolving state legal industry, marijuana businesses need all the services that any industry needs, including tax returns, sales tax returns, property tax returns, back-office accounting services, payroll, and end-of-year tax returns. Some states require annual audits of growers and marijuana retailers. In this chapter, based on a BVR webinar, Jim Marty, CPA/ABV, MS, discusses the unique aspects of a marijuana dispensary's financial records.

* * *

Exhibit 1. Gross Profit for the Medical Marijuana Industry

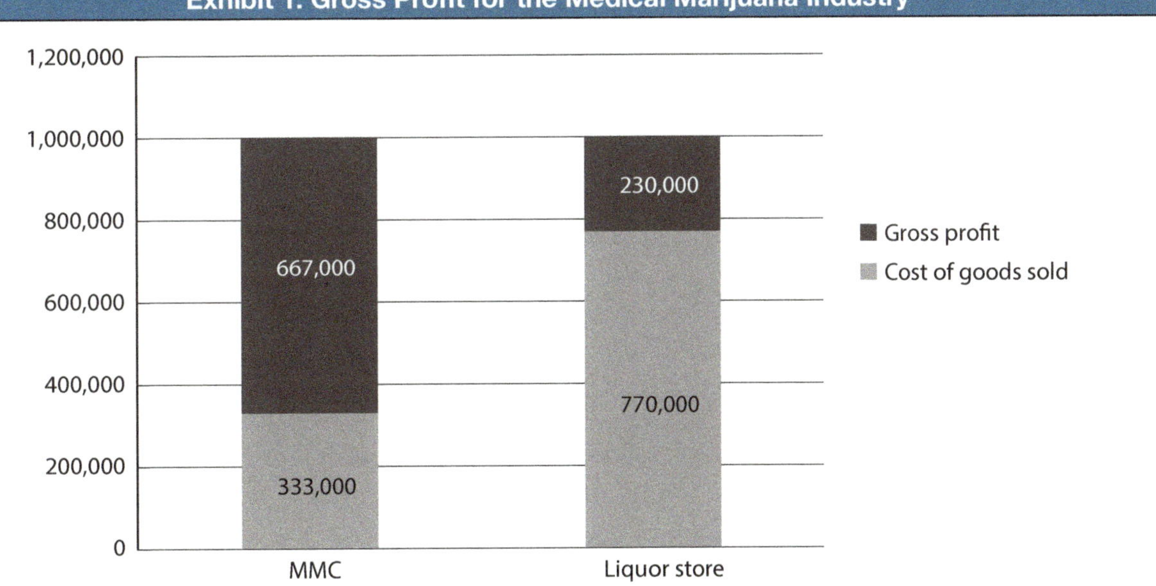

In our efforts to understand how the marijuana industry functions financially, can we compare it to another industry, such as liquor stores? Liquor stores typically operate at about a 23% profit margin; the marijuana industry has much higher margins (see Exhibit 1). A pound of marijuana sells for approximately $3,000 or more. It costs about $1,000 to grow a pound of marijuana, including warehouse rent, utilities, nutrients, and labor. Some growers are gaining great efficiencies in their gardens and grow for closer to $500 a pound, although some are less efficient and are growing for $1,500 a pound. But, as a rule of thumb, if you grow it for $1,000 a pound, you can sell it at retail for $3,000. The benchmark in Colorado dispensaries is selling an eighth of an ounce to consumers for $25. The average amount a person who goes into a dispensary spends is close to $100.

Exhibit 2 reflects how the IRS generally views an illegal business versus a legal business. The left-hand side is familiar: sales, less cost of goods, which is gross profit, less overhead, bringing you to net income before taxes. After taxes is the net income. Notice, in the second column of the exhibit, there is a blank box for overhead.

Exhibit 2. IRS's View of an Illegal Versus a Legal Business

Legal Business	Illegal Business
Sales	Sales
Costs of goods sold	Costs of goods sold
Gross profit	Gross profit
Overhead	
Net income before taxes	Net income before taxes
Net income	Net income

If you apply a 40% tax rate to the gross profit of $667,000, as indicated in Exhibit 3, the effective tax rate is about 63% instead of 40%. You cannot deduct the $250,000 of retail overhead. If you apply the same rules to a liquor store, the owner takes home only $13,000 on a million-dollar small liquor store.

Exhibit 3. Tax on Gross Profit

	Medical Marijuana $	Liquor Store $
Sales	1,000,000	1,000,000
Cost of goods sold	333,000	770,000
Gross profit (GP)	667,000	230,000
Retail overhead	250,000	125,000
Income taxes on GP at 40%	266,800	92,000
Net income after taxes	150,200	13,000
Effective tax rate	63.98%	

This makes the marijuana industry very different, and, therefore, the advice you give is going to be the opposite of what you would normally give. If you are going to tax medical marijuana, people are going to have less of it. Dispensaries have very small retail footprints because the rent for the retail space is not deductible. Advertising is not deductible either, nor are employee wages unless for cultivation.

One business model that works well if the business is zoned properly is to have a small retail space in front of the warehouse. Think of a factory outlet store for a bread factory. Maybe there are 60,000 square feet of grow space and 2,000 square feet of retail dispensary; that means 98% of the rent and utilities will be deductible.

One argument litigated recently in Tax Court was over whether, since medical marijuana dispensaries are state-licensed in Colorado, they are able to deduct their retail overhead. That is, did a state-licensed marijuana business meet the definition of "trafficking"? In *Olive v. Commissioner*, the 9th Circuit Court of Appeals, on July 9, 2015, agreed with the IRS that marijuana dispensaries cannot deduct business expenses and must pay taxes on 100% of their gross income. Thus, at least for now, IRC Section 280E does indeed apply to the medical marijuana industry in Colorado.

Let's look at the books of a typical medical marijuana center (MMC)—a dispensary. Sales tax returns help report the revenue. As more states legalize marijuana, it is a good idea that the MMC be subject to sales tax to create a revenue stream and help legitimize the industry. Many states view marijuana as a nutritional supplement, like vitamins. Vitamins are subject to sales tax, and so marijuana falls into the category of a nutritional supplement rather than a prescription drug.

Several companies offer point-of-sale (POS) software systems specifically designed for the industry. These systems provide the necessary documentation for the sales tax returns. Auditors check sales tax returns and use the reports from the POS system to back up the sales.

However, the sales tax returns are not going to equal what goes to the bank because dispensaries don't always deposit their cash. The legal marijuana industry is new, cash-based, and federally illegal, so establishing a banking relationship can be difficult. Dispensary sales will likely be higher than what has been deposited to the bank.

Since dispensary owners pay their landlords in cash, the landlord should get a Form 1099 at the end of the year. Building out a garden can cost anywhere from $50,000 to $200,000 to $3 million, with all the lights and heating and air conditioning. Many times, these garden build-outs are paid in cash, making 1099 reporting important.

Business expenses. In the eyes of the federal government, the cost of growing the plants for the illegal drug is all deductible, while the legal part—rent, payroll, utilities for anything associated with the retail—is not. The reasoning is based on constitutional grounds. The IRS defines taxable income as sales less cost of goods sold, and all deductions after cost of goods sold are at the discretion of Congress. Some people might have a different opinion, but the point is that at this time all the costs of growing marijuana are deductible. All the costs associated with running a retail dispensary are not deductible. For this reason, job descriptions are very important. We get copies of the 1099s and W-2s and have the client write job descriptions on them. There are essentially three jobs: garden, retail, and administration. Only the garden labor is deductible.

Other costs unique to the industry are state and local licensing fees, which can range from $20,000 to $50,000 a year. The IRS has a reasonableness test to build up or build down from costs of goods sold up to sales. The IRS has allowed some of those costs using a ratio analysis and reasonableness test. Look at your cost of goods sold and figure out what your sales should be. The IRS is still learning about the industry. For example, you may have to explain to the IRS that you can't figure out sales by counting the number of plants because the yields vary.

There are a number of items to address on the initial tax return, as there are in any industry. Is the owner a farmer or is it a manufacturer? Many states, such as Colorado, have tax credits that are allowed in industrial areas. I use Business Code 621399, which is, on the IRS tables, for miscellaneous health practitioners.

The Colorado Department of Revenue and the IRS define "inventory" as what is dried, weighed, bagged, and ready to go to the dispensary for sale. In other words, the plants in the ground have no inventory value, much like a farmer's corn crop is all expensed. Only when it is dried, weighed, and bagged do we assign it value. We value it at the estimated cost to grow times the estimated weight. The inventory might be at the MMC, at the retail center, or still at the warehouse. Then the question is: "Can you use Section 263A?" This is an undecided issue right now.

An article by Professor Edward Roche (University of Denver, Sturm College of Law) covers §263A in detail.[1] If retail overhead is not deductible, doesn't §263A help? Section 263A is usually an anti-taxpayer provision because it builds up ending inventory. The higher the ending inventory, the higher the net income on which you have to pay tax. The IRS makes all of the retail overhead nondeductible. In this industry, we love §263A because you don't have that much retail overhead left. On Jan. 1, 2014, the Colorado legislature began allowing dispensaries to deduct all of their retail at the state level.

Using a labor component, you can have 80% of your labor in the garden because you have to grow your own. This means that you can move 80% of retail overhead up into cost of goods sold and then a little slice goes up to ending inventory. However, the IRS has told me, "We think Professor Roche is wrong. You cannot use a §263A to make a nondeductible expense deductible."

Beginning for tax years in 2014, §280E is no longer an issue in Colorado. Colorado 2014 tax returns now have a line for deducting expenses denied at the federal level for marijuana businesses. Interestingly, California only denies §280E deductions for those convicted of a drug trafficking crime.

In January 2015, the IRS's chief counsel issued a memorandum clarifying the service's position on the federal taxation of state legal cannabis businesses. The details of this memo are covered in Chapter 5 of this report. The short version is that the IRS will strictly enforce §280E by denying all retail deductions and §263A cannot be used to mitigate the effects on taxable income.

We get representation letters for some of my clients similar to what you do in a reviewed financial statement. Form 8275 is very helpful because it protects the practitioner as well as the client from penalties if you disclose on the tax return what you are doing.

1 Edward J. Roche Jr., "Federal Income Taxation of Medical Marijuana Businesses," *Tax Lawyer*, 66, No. 2, (2013). 13-38. Available at http://bit.ly/1xIVfK8.

Balance sheet. A typical MMC balance sheet with an optional premises cultivation operation (OPC) has assets that are typically cash, inventory, and fixed assets and security deposits. You will see fixed assets if there is a grow operation—anywhere from $50,000 to $3 million in lights, build-out, air conditioning, and electrical panels. In fact, one of the first things owners who rent a warehouse do is upgrade the electrical grid. One of my clients said, "If we move out of this warehouse, we are taking everything with us including the electrical panel." So I can use a seven-year life on that.

Look for large security deposits on the balance sheet because landlords require them in this industry. It is not uncommon to see a $50,000 security deposit.

Consider a 15-year life and bonus depreciation. If you want to accelerate your depreciation because your garden depreciation is deductible, your retail depreciation is not. This is very much a startup industry, so we will elect out of bonus appreciation and do a slow straight line to preserve those deductions for the future, when we can use those deductions, or maybe we just don't need them, and we are trying to attract new partners. We can say we have this $3 million we are about to write off; if you become a partner, you can get a piece of that, or even a special allocation of that depreciation.

The liabilities that you will see on a balance sheet are sales taxes payable, payroll taxes payable, and accounts payable. You will most likely not see bank loans, but you will see loans from family members. Of course, those should be documented so you can handle them properly. With a typical $2 million garden build-out, you will have a lot of tax losses that can be valuable. Are the loans recourse or nonrecourse? We have had clients take a nonrecourse loan and make it recourse so that they get basis and take the deductions and the losses.

Regulators want to know where that capital came from, so you should have good documentation on loans and how the business was capitalized to get it started. They are interested in keeping the black market out of the industry, which is why they are very curious about where the money came from.

It is the same with equity, so document your sources. It is not uncommon to have a partnership tax return with 10 partners—many of whom are difficult to track. To ensure accuracy, we issue a draft of the return. We tell them to make sure we got all their names, addresses, Social Security numbers, and percentage of ownership (which changes all the time). Obviously, get documentation for capital contributions and changes of ownership.

Income statement. Tie sales to the sales tax returns. Make sure your clients report both their wholesale and retail sales on their tax returns because the states and cities are very interested in that. As previously addressed, sales tax returns are very helpful when the IRS looks for unreported income.

In a discussion with an IRS agent, I asked, "Do the sales equal the 12 sales tax returns? The client signed those sales tax returns under penalty of perjury." The IRS agent said, "Well, they signed the tax return under penalty of perjury, too, and I am here, aren't I?" The IRS really wants to see the proper documentation of backup, the income and expenses.

The IRS has accepted verbal testimony: "I spent a lot of money buying pounds of marijuana for my dispensary. I don't have any receipts. But I can tell you that my average cost per pound was this." It is no longer an issue now that our dispensaries grow most of their marijuana. There is no place for 1099s in the current regulatory system. Growers should not get a 1099 if they are working in the warehouse. They have not applied for a license, and they should be employees.

If the goal of regulation was to put black market growers out of business, bring them into the light, and have them get W-2s, Colorado's system has worked beautifully—almost all of the growers in the state are on W-2 wages.

It is important to categorize all costs of growing in the garden in cost of goods sold (COGS). Warehouse rent and utilities are the major costs of growing. Other supplies include clones—almost nothing is grown from seed—plant nutrients, and soil. Overhead related to the garden should really be minimal—cell phones, some automobile, legal and accounting, which are not deductible.

Depreciation on items with short lives, such as lights, should be posted to COGS. I recommend putting depreciation and COGS even on a Schedule C because you don't want to have classification issues unless there is an audit. One of my first audits said I could only take COGS. I replied that is appreciation on Schedule C even though it is down on the depreciation line. That really relates to the garden. I prevailed on the issue, but after that we force our depreciation up into cost of goods sold even on Schedule C's.

The IRS has been pretty generous on what it calls COGS. It has allowed packaging materials, transportation expenses, and moving the product around. The agency will enforce §280E, but it will also allow you to put as much as you can into COGS. I know certain penalties kick in when the change of the tax is over $5,000, and the penalties can be onerous. I have had significant changes in tax returns that I have not prepared where I just help with the audit. There have been minimal, if any, penalties, and just interest. The IRS wants to get these cases off its desk and closed. It doesn't want to clog up appeals and the tax courts.

However, since the chief counsel's memorandum came out in January 2015, the IRS has taken a harder line on what can be deducted as a cost of goods sold.

Are partnership and Schedule C's better than S corps? C corps are turning out to be a very favorable form of entity in this industry. If the IRS says you shouldn't have deducted all these millions of dollars' worth of overhead, it is going to assess you a couple million dollars in taxes. If the MMC is an LLC or an S corp, you would have to file personal bankruptcy to get rid of that tax assessment. So C corps are becoming a better deal. With an S corp, if you have a W-2 and you have a reasonable salary, that W-2 may not be deductible. That is also true of guaranteed payments in a partnership.

There are more examples of how §280E conflicts with other areas of the tax code. Is there a basis issue for third-party loans? A partnership may have more flexibility on allocating profits and losses than a C corp that can produce double taxation on dividends.

Selling expenses. Selling expenses are not deductible, even if you are using §263A. We have not done much with R&D credits, but, if you are honoring §280E, be aware that it does apply to credits as well. Advertising and cannabis consultants could be considered selling costs and therefore nondeductible under §280E and not able to be allocated under §263A.

The IRS really seems to be taking a hard line with this industry, and it is still working to understand it. Nevertheless, it is important to know how to handle the MMC's financial statements in a way that is suitable for your client and satisfactory for the IRS.

Jim Marty, *CPA/ABV, MS, of Bridge West LLC, can be reached at jmarty@jimmarty.com and 303-651-0304.*

8. Four Value Drivers for a Marijuana Dispensary

Legal marijuana dispensaries often face a variety of complex business issues, including shareholder agreements, attempts at private placement, investment strategies, and trademark and copyright protection. Dispensaries that have dealt with these issues are more attractive to potential buyers. BVR spoke with Hilary Bricken, lead attorney with the Canna Law Group, about what buyers look for when acquiring a marijuana dispensary.

BVR: *From your experience, what drives value in a marijuana dispensary?*

Hilary Bricken: I find that the value drivers in a marijuana dispensary business fall into four areas.

1. *State regulatory regimes and how the feds perceive them.*

The federal government's priorities were set forth in a memo by U.S. Deputy Attorney General James Cole on Aug. 29, 2013.[1] A potential buyer is taking on a large liability when dealing with a seller who doesn't know about this memo. In fact, it should be a red flag because sellers who are unaware of state regulations and federal enforcement policies are likely not developing best practices and could be undertaking activities that run afoul of state and local laws as well as federal policies.

Offending dispensaries will almost always be found out because the buyer will check the business's track record with the state licensing authority and its reputation in the marijuana industry to ensure that the transaction is lawful under state law.

In addition, financial institutions will be extremely apprehensive about providing banking and insurance services to marijuana dispensaries until more regulatory regimes are in place. Of course, it depends on the state in which you reside and the regulatory regime under which you're operating.

1 www.justice.gov/iso/opa/resources/3052013829132756857467.pdf.

2. *Contracts, leases, and vendor relationships.*

Long-term contracts are a boon to any buyer. These contracts are common in states such as Washington and Colorado, where transparent, candid distribution and real lines of business exist. Retailers—at least in the state of Washington because they can't vertically integrate—will want to lock those producers and processors into long-term contracts to ensure that they always, always have product on the shelf.

The length of the seller's lease is also important. If the federal government shuts down a dispensary, one of the first things it will typically do is issue a notice of asset forfeiture to that dispensary's landlord. For example, Harborside Health Center in Oakland, Calif., the largest dispensary in the United States, went through the issue in federal court in California. When the Department of Justice tried to shut down the dispensary, one of the first things it did was threaten the landlord with seizure of the building. (*Editor's note: This case was dropped in May 2016*). For a dispensary owner to have a long-term lease, it means that the landlord is comfortable with the risk, the landlord has run the idea by the bank, and the bank has decided not to foreclose on the mortgage or is comfortable with the tenant. This situation is rare but extremely valuable because it can take a long time to find a viable property with a willing landlord.

Vendor relationships are also important. Existing contracts with emerging market players who are developing branding and identity will lend more value and credibility to a dispensary than doing business with vendors that don't have a good track record or have multiple administrative violations.

3. *The value of intellectual property.*

Does the dispensary have any registered trademarks? What are those trademarks for, and are they locked down and well policed? For example, does the dispensary have trademarks under state law that directly encompass its ability to distribute product? Or is the trademark merely for ancillary services but registered with the United States Patent and Trademark Office?

How strong is the dispensary's branding? A strong and protected brand can add immense value to a company. For example, Mirth Provisions in Seattle has an intelligent branding strategy. It is producing a cold-brew coffee infused with marijuana, which received a lot of play on Fox, CNN, "The Tonight Show Starring Jimmy Fallon," and multiple media outlets. Shops in Colorado were running out of product in the first couple of months. My colleague Alison Malsbury has a blog post with more information.[2]

Dispensaries that have registered a state law trademark for the names of their strains are more attractive acquisition targets. An article in the *Chicago Tribune* points out that the right strain name can make all the difference.[3] Note that, contrary to what some lawyers are claiming, the United States does not have regional trademarks, nor is it possible to register a strain name at the federal level. You should be registering your strain trademarks with the applicable state.

2 www.cannalawblog.com/client-fridays-mirth-provisions-hits-it-big-with-branding/.
3 www.chicagotribune.com/news/la-fi-marijuana-names-20140711-story.html#page=1.

As with many products, some dispensary owners build exclusive relationships with their vendors, and a buyer will want to know who the vendors are and how long they've been your vendor. For example, a buyer may want to know whether the seller has Dixie Elixirs on the shelf because the product has great household name recognition.

The market's going to shake out, and the novelty of a product will eventually wear off. Nonetheless, the truly talented growers and businesspeople will emerge and remain strong over time. But, certainly in the first few months of the marketplace, you will want to have those vendors coming to you routinely. If they default on a contract, you will want to be able to punish them accordingly.

Of course, there's still an entrenched social stigma against marijuana, and business owners have to watch where they step. It's a combination of stigma and federal prohibition that really limits the bounds of where dispensaries can go with branding. While the business climate is beginning to change, it's still somewhat immature, essentially holding back the growth of a legitimate cannabis marketplace. I've stood by that position for a long time, and it's likely going to continue to be that way until federal prohibition is rescinded.

4. *Location, location, location.*

We had a client who won three lottery retail spaces in the city of Seattle under I-502, which is our adult/recreational use law. There are only 21 licenses in Seattle, and the 200-plus dispensaries in the Seattle area will likely get whittled down into these very lucrative 21. There is inherent value in these three spots because of the exclusivity. This particular client was able to sell a business interest in one of those locations for $1 million flat—not having done a day of business—just based on the fact of exclusivity and location.

BVR: *What are the main business disputes you are seeing within the marijuana industry?*

HB: Litigation is definitely an emerging area in the marijuana industry that is picking up speed. Initially, most litigation took place between private businesses and state and local governments regarding allegations of overregulation and/or local bans of marijuana businesses. Now, as states have begun to clarify and reform their marijuana laws, municipal and state litigation has significantly dropped off. And, as the industry develops and matures, we are seeing more partnership disputes, contract breach claims of all kinds (e.g., vendor contracts, loan agreements, service agreements, etc.), and commercial landlord/tenant disputes and lawsuits. Thus far, state courts have been willing to uphold marijuana contracts pursuant to "robust state regulations." I have not seen a single contract thrown out on a theory of illegality, for example. Nonetheless, I believe that more parties, like most litigants, look to settle their disputes outside of court, both because they fear how the courts may treat marijuana business contracts and business entities and because, as mostly startup businesses, most of these organizations cannot afford a full-blown lawsuit going all the way to trial.

Editor's note: Readers who value marijuana dispensaries and related businesses should follow the Canna Law Blog at www.cannalawblog.com. Its frequent and insightful posts contain valuable information on the growing cannabis industry.

9. What Are Investors Looking for in Marijuana Dispensaries?

Editor's note: Investors with hopes of striking it big are investing in the legal marijuana industry. In fact, the ArcView Investor Network, almost six years old, consists of 500-plus high-net-worth accredited investors with eyes on cannabis businesses. Troy Dayton, ArcView CEO, shared his insight on investing in marijuana dispensaries.

* * *

BVR: *How and why do investors play a role in the marijuana dispensary industry?*

Troy Dayton: A lot of dispensaries and licensed cultivators—which in many cases are the same because some states require vertical integration—are not keen on giving up equity. They are businesses with strong cash flows; there is usually limited licensing, so they're essentially being given a monopoly.

Despite the fact that they have incredible margins—almost guaranteed margins—these businesses need capital. But the owners are much more motivated to engage in high-interest loans than they are to give up equity. Currently, the top dispensaries and marijuana businesses are getting their funding through high-interest loans because payment is practically guaranteed if they get their licenses. In fact, we're seeing loans with 14% to 20% interest getting approved, and the businesses are paying them off in two or three years.

There are also regulatory reasons why loans are common. In some states, these businesses are required to be nonprofit. In a nonprofit, you can't sell equity, but you can do high-interest loans. Other states have residency requirements; you have to be a resident of that state to be an investor but not to loan money.

Many businesses convert the loan into equity when it's possible to do so, for example, if the laws change in a way that allows for equity or if the lenders become residents of a state that allows them to have equity.

BVR: *What do investors consider before giving a dispensary a loan?*

TD: It really depends on the state and its regulatory environment. If it's a tough regulatory environment where the business has to show that it has millions of dollars in the bank to even apply and it needs a superdetailed business plan that meets with lots of regulations and has to undergo deep background checks, then the state is essentially doing a lot of the work for the investor. In other words, the fact that somebody has a license is often enough for the investors to say, "All right, I'm in," because they know how hard it would be to get that license. Their due diligence isn't nearly as stringent as the state's. Conversely, investors need to do a lot more due diligence on the actual operators in states that are looser, such as California.

Investors look for a team that knows how to scale business operations, knows cannabis, and has good legal representation. These qualities are hard to find because, to know how to grow cannabis on a large scale, you generally need to have been in the underground economy or worked in one of the few well-regulated medical cannabis states on large-scale cultivation. It's hard to find those people. Many dispensaries are working with consulting firms that have knowledge about scaling, cultivation, and operation.

Industry competition is defined at the state level, and it's not so much about the operators as it is about the competitive framework. For example, Illinois is a tough state because it has a very stringent medical cannabis law. So, at least in the short run, those businesses are unlikely to be particularly profitable. But businesses already in operation will have an advantage if and when the law gets expanded.

So, although these businesses in stringent states are going to take a long time before they are profitable, investors are banking on the expansion of the law. On the other hand, there might be other, more immediately lucrative, opportunities in states such as Nevada or Arizona, which have broader laws.

BVR: *What can business appraisers learn from investors in cannabis businesses?*

TD: Investors value marijuana dispensaries differently than other businesses because the opportunity is different. In most cases, these valuations are completely unrelated to the fundamentals. People are investing in future potential, so the real test is: Does the business have the kind of team that is going to win the day? Investors will consider whether a company can and will take things to the next level in five to 10 years rather than what it's currently doing or what its current sales are.

In addition, you have to rethink how you value a business run by an entrepreneur. Being an entrepreneur in this space necessitates that you're also an activist, a philanthropist, and somebody who is challenging taboos in society.

Of course, it's very hard to find comparables, and buyers, for the most part, are overpaying for companies. You need to decide now whether you are willing to overpay. If you wait because you don't want to overpay, you're going to spend a lot more for even less later.

BVR: What do you think the future holds for the cannabis industry?

TD: Cannabis is a fast-growing industry in this country. We are seeing incredible business activity and a big shift in public opinion that is leading to an expanding marketplace, the likes of which we've just never seen before.

So is it a bubble? Yes, in some cases, it is a bubble, but it's a bubble that I think will not pop until 2020 or 2021. People are investing and building ancillary businesses in the hope of a huge payout when the government changes federal law and allows the states to do what they want on cannabis, which we predict will happen in 2019 or 2020. And, when that happens, the multinationals are going to acquire all of these companies, and there's going to be a payday. We'll see cannabis companies making $50 million, $100 million a year, engaging in IPOs, and getting listed on Nasdaq.

And the key thing is you don't have to violate federal law to be involved in this sector. I'm involved in this sector; I don't violate federal law. Lots of businesses benefit from this boom, and there are many ways to be involved. For example, ancillary businesses include packaging, point-of-sale software, growing equipment, consumption devices, live events, media, industrial hemp, and more.

10. Medical Marijuana Dispensary Financial Report From BizMiner

This chapter provides a wealth of financial information on medical marijuana dispensaries in the United States. The information, sourced from the *BizMiner Industry Financial Report* (available at www.bvresources.com/bizminer), provides you with key financial data, including financial statements and financial ratios, to assist you in benchmarking one dispensary's performance against others. The topics covered in this chapter include:

- Income-expense statement (dollar-based);
- Income-expense statement (percentage-based);
- Balance sheet (dollar-based);
- Balance sheet (percentage-based);
- Sources and uses of funds;
- Financial ratios: cash flow solvency;
- Financial ratios: profitability;
- Financial ratios: efficiency debt risk; and
- Financial ratios: turnover.

Time series and sales classes. The financial reports included in this chapter analyze calendar years 2013 through 2015, as displayed in Exhibit 1.

The sales classes applied in this report are broken down as follows:

- $500,000-$999,999;
- $1 million-$2.49 million;
- $2.5 million-$4.99 million;
- $5 million-$9.99 million; and
- $10 million-$24.99 million.

Exhibit 1. Number of Businesses Analyzed for This Report

Year	Number of Businesses
2013	494
2014	568
2015	488

Income-expense statement (dollar-based and percentage-based). Exhibit 2 details the income-expense statements in dollars for marijuana medical dispensaries (MMDs) over the past three years, while Exhibit 3 details the same in percentages. Dollar-based sales and other dollar-based data in this report reflect averages for sales of the industry segment, not total industrywide averages. As a result, sales levels may vary from year to year, depending on the mix of firms that fall within the selected segment. Explanation of categories is shown below.

Business revenue. Business revenue includes receipts from core business operations. Interest income and other income (such as rents and royalties) are generally detailed separately below operating income. While business revenue is separated from interest income for most classifications, business revenue includes interest income from the private sector where it is central to financial industry operations, including finance and insurance (NAICS 52xxxx except NAICS 5242xx—Insurance Brokers and Other Insurance Activities; Real Estate-Rental-Leasing (53xxxx); and Management of Companies and Enterprises (55xxxx)).

Exhibit 2. Income and Expense (Profit and Loss in Dollars)

	2013	2014	2015
Business revenue	1,017,323	1,014,835	1,195,204
Cost of sales	629,413	659,449	728,368
Cost of sales—labor portion	7,906	8,399	11,308
Gross margin	387,910	355,386	466,836
Officers comp.	54,943	53,386	68,849
Salary—wages	83,229	77,198	96,703
Rent	45,231	38,107	41,442
Taxes paid	17,572	17,067	19,796
Advertising	12,555	9,476	15,946
Benefits—pensions	9,401	6,286	9,362
Repairs	5,779	2,914	5,142
Bad debt	879	1,241	870
Sales, general, admin & misc.	56,877	56,336	71,020
EBITDA	101,444	93,375	137,706
Amortization, depreciation, depletion	9,726	7,093	7,315
Operating expenses	296,192	269,104	336,445
Operating income	91,718	86,282	130,391
Interest income	809	707	154
Interest expense	3,131	2,038	2,515
Other income	3,006	3,687	4,937
Pretax net profit	92,402	88,638	132,967
Income tax	19,667	18,388	35,106
After tax net profit	72,735	70,250	97,861
Discretionary owner earnings	137,404	130,729	174,025

Cost of sales. Cost of sales includes materials and labor involved in the direct delivery of a product or service. Other costs are included in the cost of sales to the extent that they are involved in bringing goods to their location and condition ready to be sold. Nonproduction overhead such as development costs may be attributable to the cost of goods sold. The costs of services provided consist primarily of personnel directly engaged in providing the service, including supervisory personnel and attributable overhead.

Gross margin. Gross margin represents direct operating expenses plus net profit. In addition to the labor portion of cost of sales, wage costs are reflected in the officers' compensation and wages-salary line items. In many cases, sales, general, and administrative (SG&A) costs also include some overhead, administrative, and supervisory wages.

Rent. Rent covers the rental cost of any business property, including land, buildings, and equipment.

Taxes paid. Taxes paid includes payroll and other paid-in tax items but not business income taxes due for the period. Although it can be calculated in many ways and is a controversial measure,

Exhibit 3. Income and Expense (Profit and Loss as a Percentage)

	2013	2014	2015
Business revenue	100.0%	100.0%	100.0%
Cost of sales	61.87%	64.98%	60.94%
Cost of sales—labor portion	0.78%	0.83%	0.95%
Gross margin	38.13%	35.02%	39.06%
Officers comp.	5.40%	5.26%	5.76%
Salary—wages	8.18%	7.61%	8.09%
Rent	4.45%	3.75%	3.47%
Taxes paid	1.73%	1.68%	1.66%
Advertising	1.23%	0.93%	1.33%
Benefits—pensions	0.92%	0.62%	0.78%
Repairs	0.57%	0.29%	0.43%
Bad debt	0.09%	0.12%	0.07%
Sales, general, admin & misc.	5.59%	5.55%	5.94%
EBITDA	9.97%	9.21%	11.53%
Amortization, depreciation, depletion	0.96%	0.70%	0.61%
Operating expenses	29.12%	26.51%	28.14%
Operating income	9.01%	8.51%	10.92%
Interest income	0.08%	0.07%	0.01%
Interest expense	0.31%	0.20%	0.21%
Other income	0.30%	0.36%	0.41%
Pretax net profit	9.08%	8.74%	11.13%
Income tax	1.93%	1.81%	2.94%
After tax net profit	7.15%	6.93%	8.19%
Discretionary owner earnings	13.51%	12.89%	14.56%

the earnings before interest expense, income tax due, depreciation, and amortization (EBITDA) adds back interest payments, depreciation, amortization, and depletion allowances and excludes income taxes due to reduce the effect of accounting decisions on the bottom line of the profit and loss statement. Since some firms utilize EBITDA to "add back" noncash and flexible expenses that may be altered through credits and accounting procedures (such as income tax), paid-in income taxes from the taxes paid line are not added back in the EBITDA calculation.

Advertising. Advertising includes advertising, promotion, and publicity for the reporting business but not on behalf of others.

Benefits-pension. Benefits-pension includes, but is not limited to, employee healthcare and retirement costs. In addition to varying proportions of overhead, administrative, and supervisory wages, some generally more minor expenses are aggregated under SG&A.

Operating expenses. Operating expenses sums the individual expense line items above, yielding the operating income or net of core business operations, when subtracted from the gross margin.

Pretax net profit. This represents net profit before income tax due. Income tax calculates the federal corporate tax rate before credits, leaving after-tax profit at the bottom line.

Discretionary owner earnings (DOE). DOE sums officer compensation, depreciation, and related noncash expenses and net profit after business taxes to represent a practical measure of total return to owners. The DOE metric is mainly used for small businesses.

Balance sheet (dollar-based and percentage-based). Exhibits 4 and 5 detail the balance sheet's averages for U.S.-based breweries. The data in this section include:

- *Cash:* Money on hand in checking, savings, or redeemable certificate accounts;
- *Receivables:* A short-term asset (to be collected within one year) in the form of accounts or notes receivable and usually representing a credit for a completed sale or loan;
- *Inventory:* The stockpile of unsold products;
- *Current assets:* The sum of a business's cash, accounts and notes receivable, inventory, prepaid expenses, and marketable securities that can be converted to cash within a single operating cycle;
- *Fixed assets:* Long-term assets such as building and machinery, net of accumulated amortization-depreciation-depletion;
- *Total assets:*[1] The sum of current assets and fixed assets such as plant and equipment;
- *Accounts payable:* Invoices due to suppliers within the current business cycle;
- *Loans/notes payable:* Loan amounts due to suppliers within the current business cycle;

1 Some legacy year asset line items are blended with the closest four-digit industry segment.

Exhibit 4. Balance Sheet (Dollar-Based)			
Assets	**2013**	**2014**	**2015**
Cash	32,137	32,664	44,208
Receivables	23,443	20,736	28,753
Inventory	67,584	62,254	86,552
Other current assets	-2,258	72	-767
Total current assets	120,906	115,726	158,746
Gross fixed assets	32,287	32,344	40,880
Accum. depreciation-amortization depltn.	11,321	11,341	14,335
Net fixed assets	20,966	21,003	26,546
Other noncurrent assets	17,857	16,526	23,361
Total assets	159,729	153,255	208,653
Liabilities			
Accounts payable	31,643	28,697	42,286
Loans/notes payable	5,359	5,062	7,957
Other current liabilities	12,208	11,824	18,427
Total current liabilities	49,210	45,583	68,669
Total long term liabilities	36,012	33,558	46,063
Total liabilities	85,222	79,141	114,733
Net worth	74,507	74,114	93,920
Total liabilities & net worth	159,729	153,255	208,653

Exhibit 5. Balance Sheet (Percentage-Based)			
Assets	**2013**	**2014**	**2015**
Cash	20.12%	21.31%	21.19%
Receivables	14.68%	13.53%	13.78%
Inventory	42.31%	40.62%	41.48%
Other current assets	-1.41%	0.05%	-0.37%
Total current assets	75.70%	75.51%	76.08%
Gross fixed assets	20.21%	21.10%	19.59%
Accum. depreciation-amortization-depltn.	7.09%	7.40%	6.87%
Net fixed assets	13.13%	13.70%	12.72%
Other noncurrent assets	11.17%	10.79%	11.20%
Total assets	100.00%	100.00%	100.00%
Liabilities			
Accounts payable	19.81%	18.72%	20.27%
Loans/notes payable	3.36%	3.30%	3.81%
Other current liabilities	7.64%	7.72%	8.83%
Total current liabilities	30.81%	29.74%	32.91%
Total long-term liabilities	22.55%	21.90%	22.08%
Total liabilities	53.36%	51.64%	54.99%
Net worth	46.64%	48.36%	45.01%
Total liabilities & net worth	100.00%	100.00%	100.00%

- *Current liabilities:* Measurable debt owed within one year, including accounts, loans and notes payable, accrued liabilities, and taxes due;
- *Long-term liabilities:* Debt that is due in more than one year, including the portion of loans and mortgages that become due after the current business cycle;
- *Total liabilities:* Current liabilities plus long-term liabilities such as notes and mortgages due over more than one year; and
- *Net worth:* Current assets plus fixed assets minus current and long-term liabilities.

Sources and uses. The "Sources and Uses of Funds" table (Exhibit 6) tests the accuracy of the balance sheet and distinguishes the sources of funds from their use. It is the basic worksheet preliminary to a formal cash flow statement examining the liquidity of a business. A multiyear industry benchmark common size balance sheet, which includes overlapped but not identical sets of firms in each year, is not well suited for the presentation of a formal cash flow analysis.

Exhibit 6. Sources and Uses of Funds

Change in:	12-13	13-14	14-15
Cash and cash equivalents	-11,637	527	11,544
Worksheet:			
Accounts receivable	914	2,707	-8,017
Inventory	4,213	5,330	-24,297
Other current assets	5,688	-2,330	839
Net fixed assets	7,931	-37	-5,543
Other noncurrent assets	-1,385	1,331	-6,835
Accounts payable	-2,841	-2,946	13,589
Loans/notes payable	-239	-297	2,895
Other current liabilities	-418	-384	6,603
Long-term debt	-10,565	-2,454	12,506
Net worth	-14,934	-393	19,806
Total sources & uses	-11,637	527	11,544
Cash: beginning period	43,774	32,137	32,664
Cash: end period	32,137	32,664	44,208
Change in cash & cash equivalents	-11,637	527	11,544

Financial ratios: cash flow solvency. Financial ratios that measure cash flow solvency are an indicator of the financial health of a business. Each ratio is described below. Exhibit 7 displays the average financial ratios for MMDs over the past three years while Exhibits 8 to 14 show the trends of these ratios over the past three years.

Accounts payable to business revenue. Accounts payable divided by annual business revenue, measuring the speed with which a company pays vendors relative to business revenue. Numbers higher than typical industry ratios suggest that the company may be using suppliers to float operations.

Current liabilities to net worth. Current liabilities divided by net worth, reflecting a level of security for creditors. The larger the ratio relative to industry norms, the less security there is for creditors.

Current liabilities to inventory. Current liabilities divided by inventory. A high ratio, relative to industry norms, suggests overreliance on unsold goods to finance operations.

Current ratio. This is the same as current assets divided by current liabilities, measuring current assets available to cover current liabilities, a test of near-term solvency. The ratio indicates to what extent cash on hand and disposable assets are enough to pay off near-term liabilities. The quick ratio is applied as a more stringent test.

Days payable. 365/(cost of sales-to-accounts payable ratio). This reflects the average number of days for each payable before payment is made.

Quick ratio. Cash plus accounts receivable, divided by current liabilities, indicating liquid assets available to cover current debt. Quick ratio is also known as the acid ratio. This is a harsher version of the current ratio, which balances short-term liabilities against cash and liquid instruments.

Total liabilities. Net worth to total liabilities divided by net worth. This ratio helps to clarify the impact of long-term debt, which can be seen by comparing this ratio with current liabilities to net worth. Creditors are concerned to the extent that total liability levels exceed net worth.

Exhibit 7. Financial Ratios: Cash Flow Solvency

	2013	2014	2015
Accounts payable: business revenue (%)	3.11	2.83	3.54
Current liabilities: inventory	0.73	0.73	0.79
Current liabilities: net worth	0.66	0.62	0.73
Current ratio	2.46	2.54	2.31
Days payable	18.35	15.88	21.19
Quick ratio	1.13	1.17	1.06
Total liabilities: net worth	1.14	1.07	1.22

Exhibit 8. Current Liabilities to Net Worth

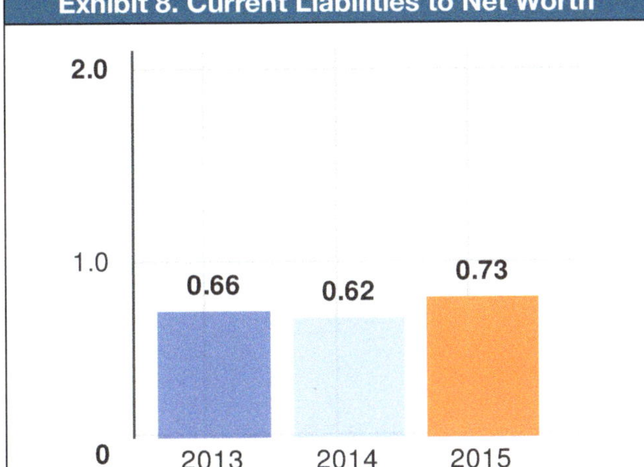

Exhibit 9. Current Liabilities to Inventory

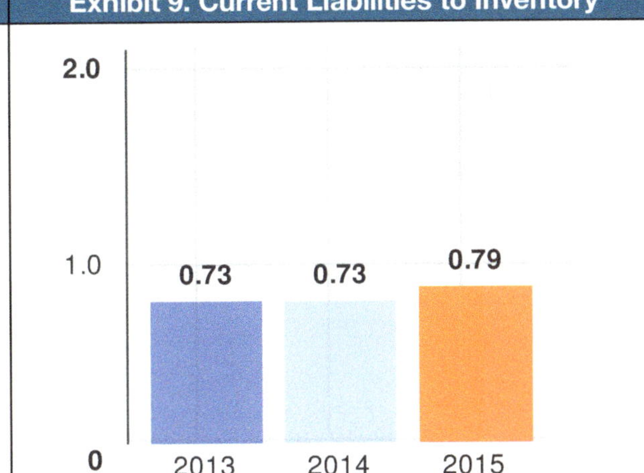

Exhibit 10. Accounts Payable to Sales (%)

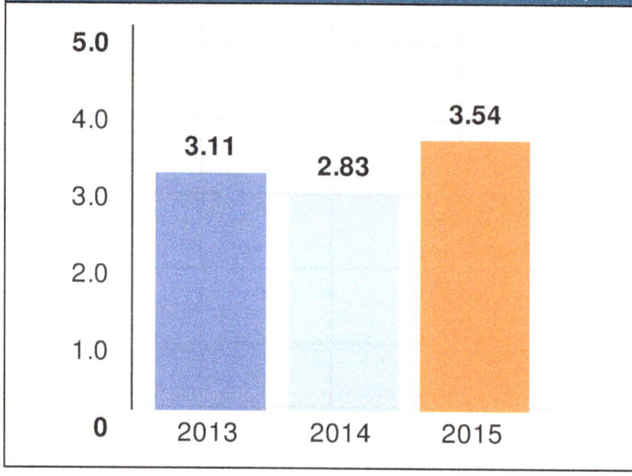

Exhibit 11. Current Ratio

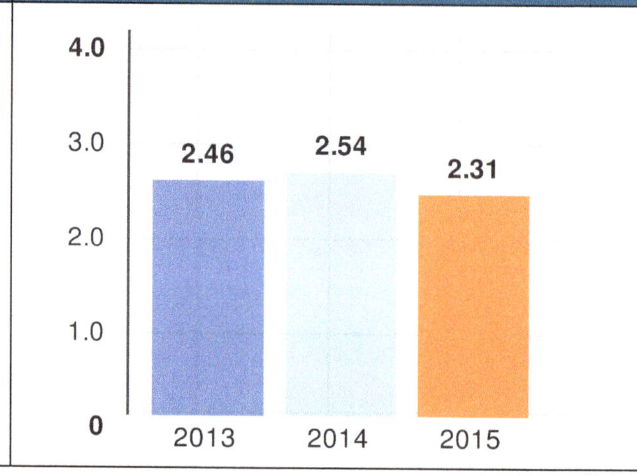

Exhibit 12. Days Payable

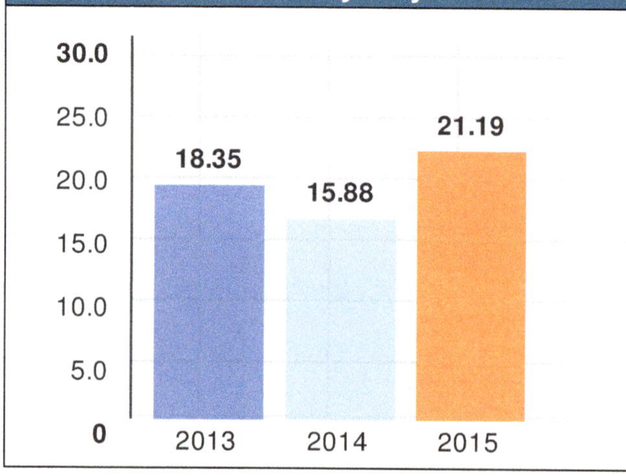

Exhibit 13. Quick Ratio

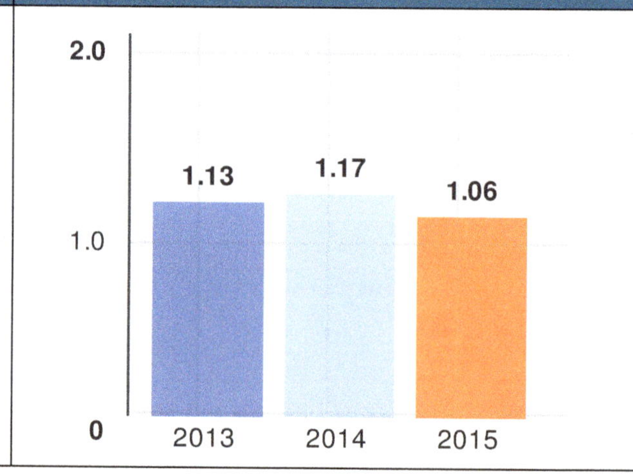

Exhibit 14. Total Liabilities to Net Worth

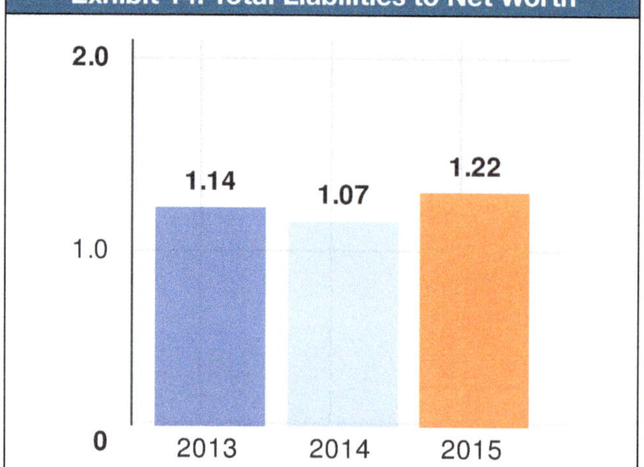

Financial ratios: profitability. Of course every business wants to know how it measures up with its peers in terms of profitability. Exhibits 15 through 19 display the average profitability for medical marijuana businesses. The five profitability measurements included in this report follow.

EBITDA to business revenue. Earnings before interest, (income) taxes due, depreciation, and amortization divided by business revenue. EBITDA to business revenue is a relatively controversial (and often criticized) metric designed to eliminate the effect of finance and accounting decisions when comparing companies and industry benchmarks. Tax credits and deferral procedures and noncash expenditures (amortization and depreciation) are not deducted from the profit equation, as are interest expenditures.

Return on assets. Pretax or after-tax net profit divided by total assets is a critical indicator of profitability. Companies that use their assets efficiently tend to show a ratio higher than the industry norm. The ratio may appear higher for small businesses due to owner compensation draws accounted as net profit.

Return on net worth. Pretax or after-tax net profit divided by net worth. This is the "final measure" of profitability to evaluate overall return. This ratio measures return relative to investment or how well a company leverages the investment. The ratio may appear higher for small businesses due to owner compensation draws accounted as net profit.

Return on business revenue. Pretax or after-tax net profit divided by annual business revenue, indicating the level of profit from each dollar of business revenue. This ratio can be used as a predictor of the company's ability to withstand changes in prices or market conditions. The ratio may appear higher for small businesses due to owner compensation draws accounted as net profit.

Discretionary owner earnings. Sums officer compensation, depreciation, and related noncash expenses and net profit after business taxes to represent a practical measure of total return to owners. This metric is mainly used for small businesses.

Exhibit 15. Financial Ratios: Profitability

	2013	2014	2015
EBITDA: Business revenue (%)	9.97	9.20	11.52
Pretax return on assets (%)	57.85	57.84	63.73
Pretax return on net worth (%)	124.02	119.60	141.57
Pretax return on business revenue (%)	9.08	8.74	11.13
After-tax return on assets (%)	45.54	45.84	46.90
After-tax return on net worth (%)	97.62	94.79	104.19
After-tax return on business revenue (%)	7.15	6.93	8.19
Discretionary owner earnings (%)	13.51	12.89	14.56

Exhibit 16. EBITDA to Business Revenue (%)

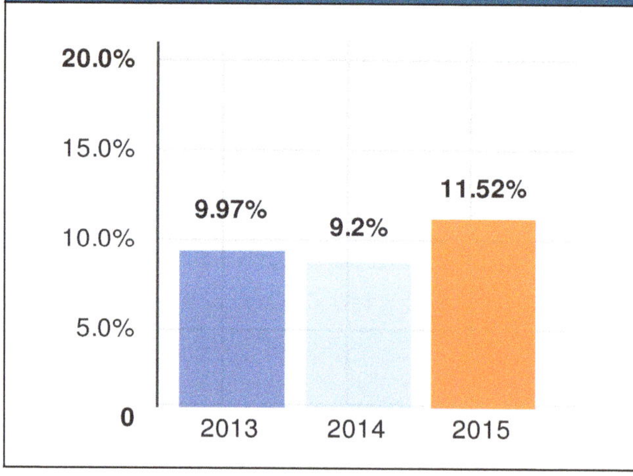

Exhibit 17. Return on Assets Pretax (%)

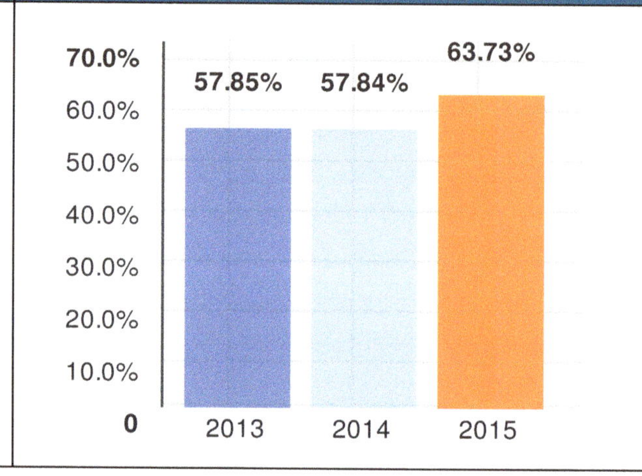

Exhibit 18. Return on Net Worth Pretax (%)

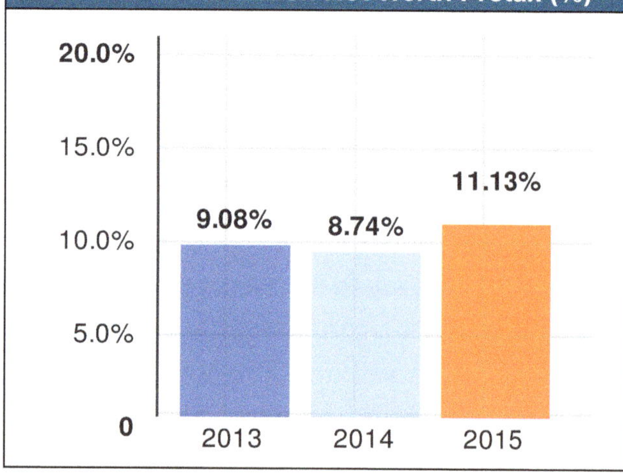

Exhibit 19. Return on Business Revenue Pretax (%)

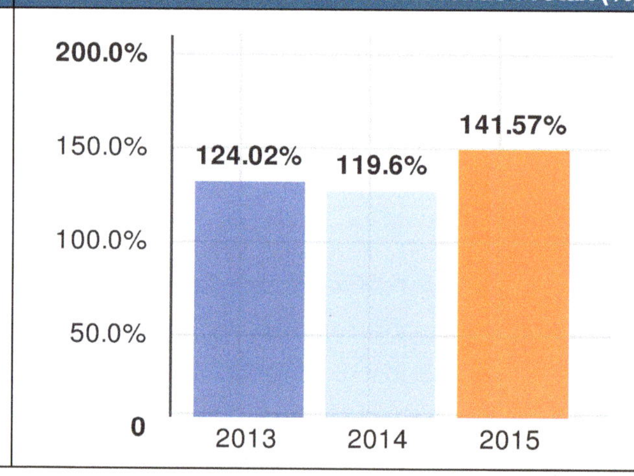

Financial ratios: efficiency debt risk. Exhibits 20 to 30 display the financial ratios for efficiency debt risk for U.S.-based MMDs, which are indicators of how well a company's resources are managed.

Assets to business revenue. Total assets divided by net business revenue, which indicates whether a company is handling too high a volume of business revenue in relation to investment. Very low percentages relative to industry norms might indicate overly conservative sales efforts or poor sales management.

Cost of sales to accounts payable. Measures the number of times payables turn over in the course of the year. High measures may indicate cash flow concerns.

Cost of sales to inventory. Reflects the number of times inventory is turned over during the course of the year. High levels can mean good liquidity or business revenue or shortages requiring better management. Low levels may indicate poor cash flow or overstocking.

Days inventory. 365/(cost of sales to inventory). The average number of days of items in inventory.

Days receivables. 365/(receivables turnover). Reflects the number of days that receivables are outstanding. Target average or lower.

Days working capital. 365/(working capital turnover). Expresses the coverage in number of days of available working capital.

EBITDA to interest expense. Earnings before interest, (income) taxes due, depreciation, and amortization divided by interest expense. Assesses financial stability by examining whether a company is at least profitable enough to pay interest expense. A ratio greater than 1.00 indicates it is. See cautions in the listing for EBITDA.

Fixed assets to net worth. Fixed assets divided by net worth. High ratios relative to the industry can indicate low working capital or high levels of debt.

Gross margin to business revenue. Pretax profits divided by annual business revenue. This is the profit ratio before product and business revenue costs, as well as taxes. This ratio can indicate the "play" in other expenses, which could be adjusted to increase the net profit margin.

Net working capital to business revenue. Net working capital divided by business revenue. This measure indicates whether a company is maintaining a reasonable level of liquidity relative to its business revenue volume. A high ratio indicates an overly conservative reliance on liquid assets, while low ratios suggest the opposite.

Loans/notes payable to net worth. The loans/notes payable portion of current liabilities divided by net worth is a measure of debt coverage.

Long-term liabilities to net worth. Long-term liabilities divided by net worth is a measure of debt coverage.

Exhibit 20. Financial Ratios: Efficiency Debt Risk

	2013	2014	2015
Assets: business revenue	0.16	0.15	0.17
Cost of sales: accounts payable	19.89	22.99	17.22
Cost of sales: inventory	9.31	10.59	8.42
Days inventory	39.19	34.46	43.37
Days receivables	8.41	7.46	8.78
Days working capital	25.72	25.23	27.51
EBITDA: interest expense	32.40	45.81	54.76
Fixed assets: net worth	0.28	0.28	0.28
Gross margin: business revenue	38.13	35.02	39.06
Net working capital: business revenue	0.07	0.07	0.08
Loans/notes payable: net worth	0.07	0.07	0.08
Long-term liabilities: net worth	0.48	0.45	0.49

Exhibit 21. Assets to Business Revenue

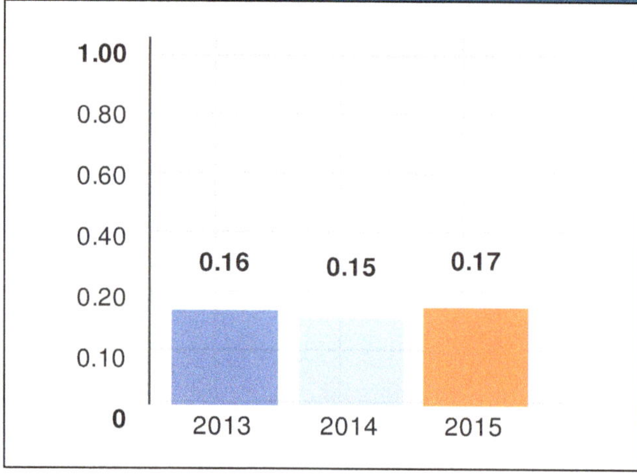

Exhibit 22. Cost of Sales to Accounts Payable

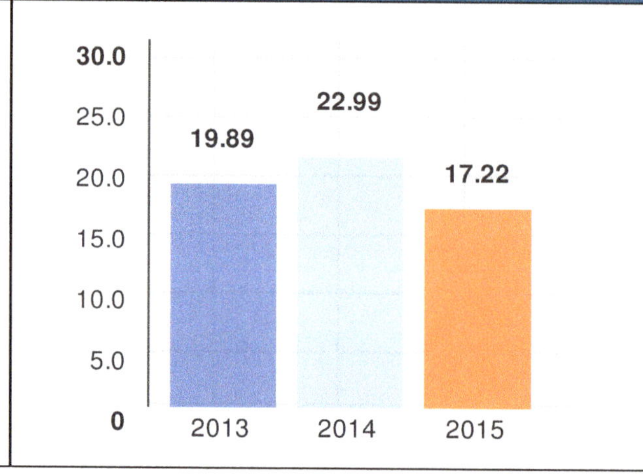

Exhibit 23. Cost of Sales to Inventory

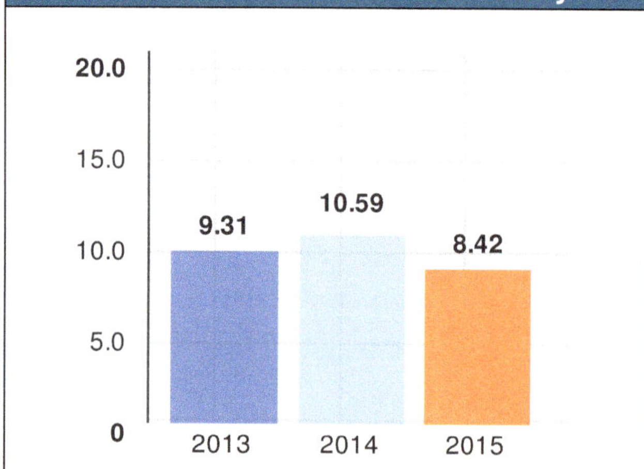

Exhibit 24. Days Inventory

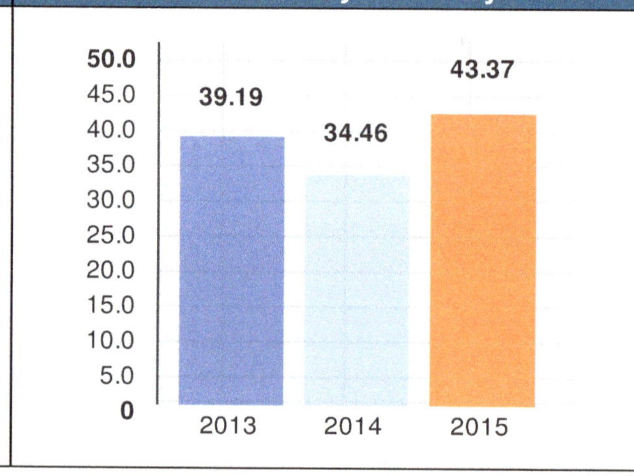

Exhibit 25. Days Receivables (X)

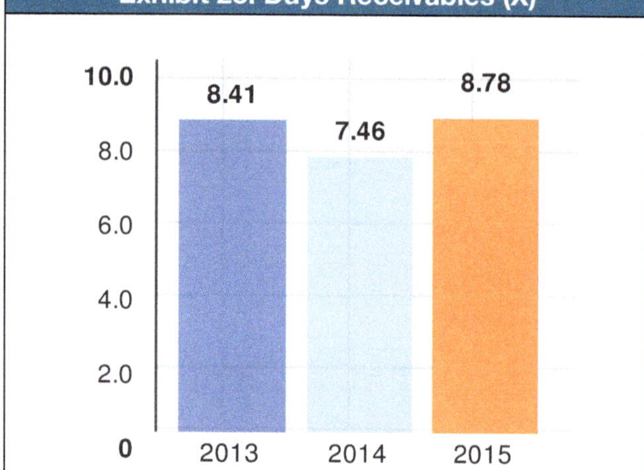

Exhibit 26. Days Working Capital

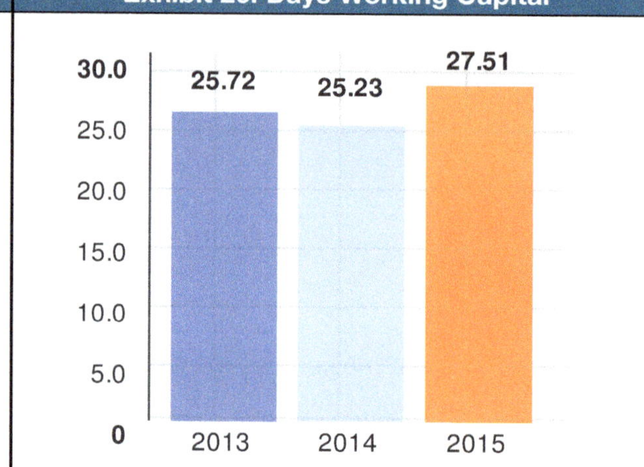

Exhibit 27. EBITDA to Interest

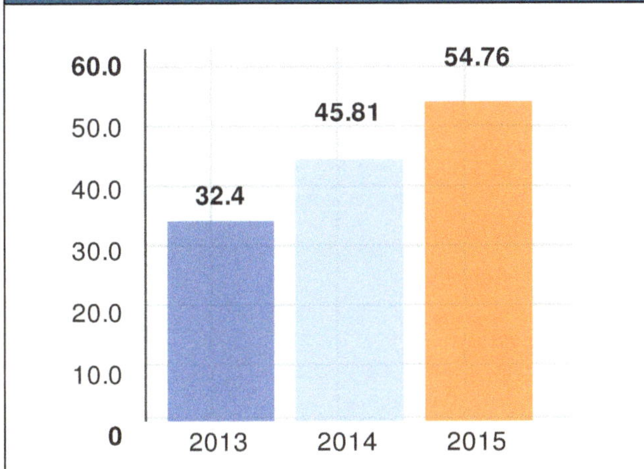

Exhibit 28. Fixed Assets to Net Worth

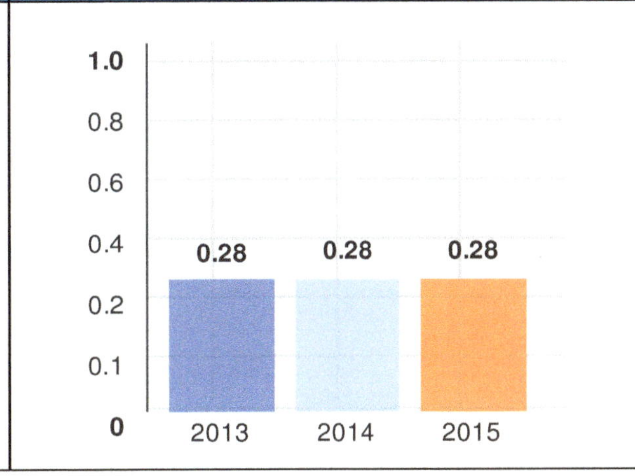

Exhibit 29. Gross Margin to Business Revenue

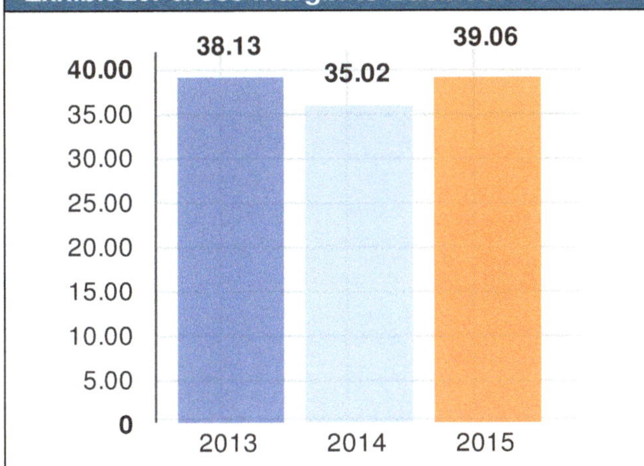

Exhibit 30. Net Working Capital to Sales

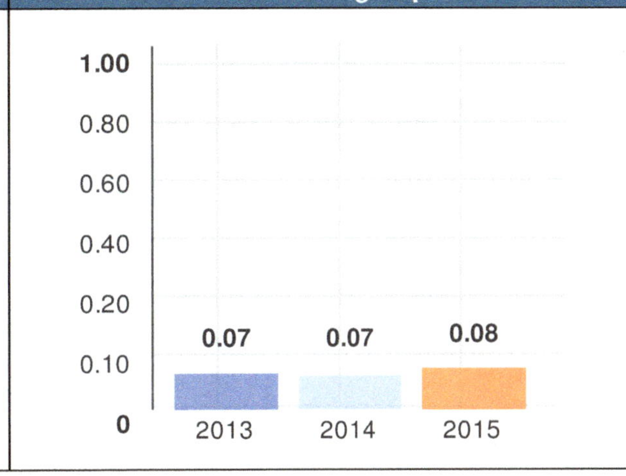

Financial ratios: turnover. Exhibits 31 to 37 display the financial ratios for turnover within several categories (see definitions below) for medical marijuana dispensaries, indicators of efficiencies in a company's assets management.

Cash turnover. Business revenue divided by cash. This measure indicates a company's efficiency in the use of cash to develop business revenue. It is a more stringent ratio than working capital turnover (below). Target at or slightly below industry level.

Current asset turnover. Business revenue divided by current assets. This is a general indicator of the efficiency of asset use. Target at or slightly below industry level.

Fixed asset turnover. Business revenue divided by fixed assets. This is an indicator of the efficiency of investment in fixed asset such as plant and equipment. Target at or slightly below industry level.

Inventory turnover. Business revenue divided by inventory. This ratio gives a picture of how quickly inventory turns over. Ratios below the industry norm suggest high levels of inventory. High ratios could indicate product levels insufficient to satisfy demand in a timely manner. Target at or slightly above industry level.

Receivables turnover. Business revenue divided by receivables. This ratio is an indicator of how efficiently invoiced sales are collected. Target at or slightly above industry level.

Total asset turnover. Business revenue divided by total assets. Target at or slightly below industry level.

Working capital turnover. Business revenue divided by net working capital (current assets minus current liabilities). Ratios higher than industry norms may indicate a strain on available liquid assets, while low ratios may suggest too much liquidity. Target at or above industry level.

Exhibit 31. Financial Ratios: Turnover

	2013	2014	2015
Cash turnover (X)	31.66	31.07	27.03
Current asset turnover	8.41	8.77	7.53
Fixed asset turnover	48.51	48.33	45.03
Inventory turnover (X)	15.05	16.30	13.81
Receivables turnover (X)	43.39	48.94	41.57
Total asset turnover (X)	6.37	6.62	5.73
Working capital turnover (X)	14.19	14.47	13.27

Exhibit 32. Cash Turnover

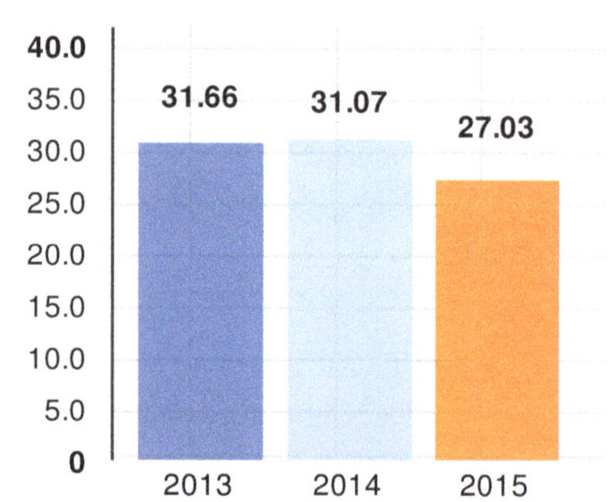

Exhibit 33. Current Asset Turnover

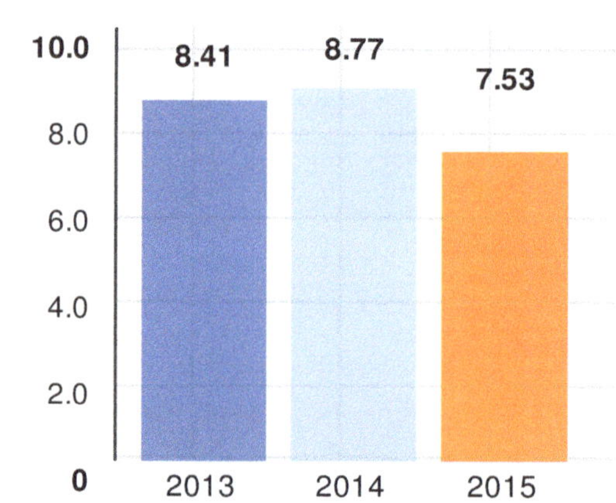

Exhibit 34. Fixed Asset Turnover

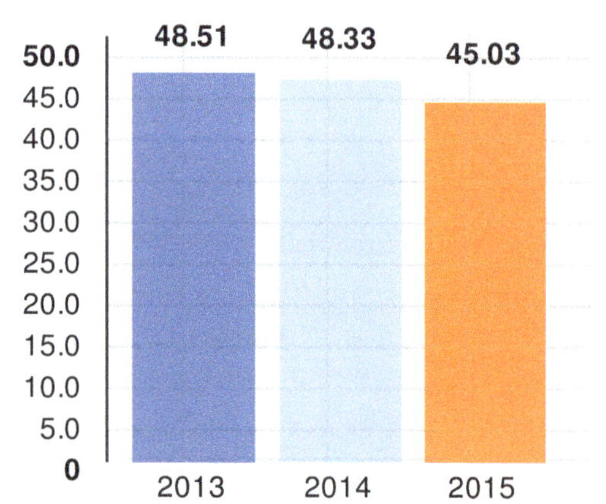

Exhibit 35. Inventory Turnover (X)

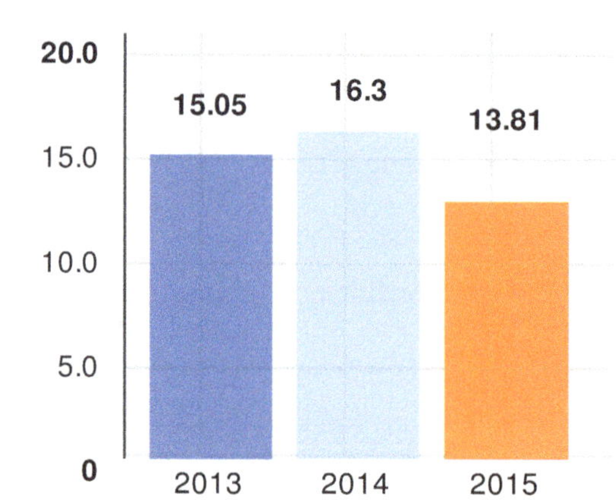

Exhibit 36. Receivables Turnover (X)

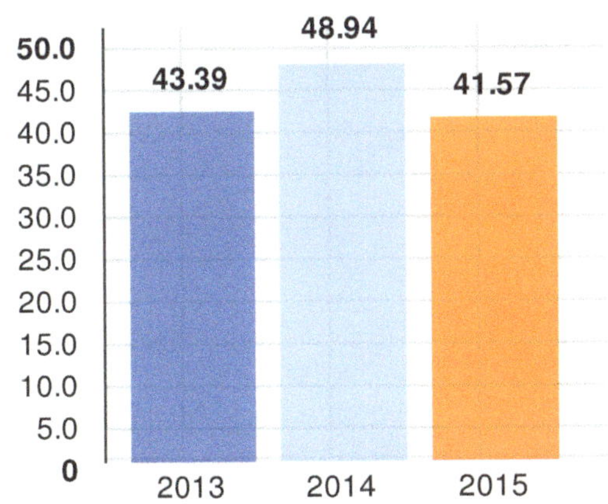

Exhibit 37. Total Asset Turnover (X)

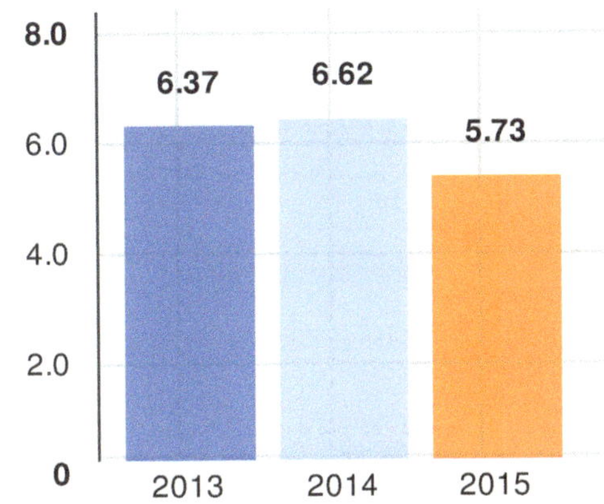

About the data. Raw data analyzed for BizMiner reports are sourced from an array of the nation's government and private statistical sources. None of these raw data sources creates the final measures reflected in BizMiner industry profiles. In total, BizMiner accesses over a billion sourced data points from 15 million business operations for each of its twice-annual updates covering a three-to-five-year time series. Historical data and BizMiner algorithms are used to inform and test projections for nonreporting firms. Data elements are sourced specifically from:

- IRS SOI Corporation Income Tax Returns;
- IRS SOI Corporation Tax Book
- IRS SOI 1040 Schedule C Income Tax Returns;
- IRS SOI Statistics of Income;
- Individual tax statistics;
- U.S. Economic Census of Manufactures;
- U.S. Census Economy Overview;
- U.S. Census Annual Survey of Manufactures;
- U.S. Census Annual Retail Trade Survey;
- U.S. Census Annual Wholesale Trade Survey;
- U.S. Census Quarterly Financial Reports;
- U.S. Census County Business Patterns;
- Bureau of Labor Statistics monthly employment reports;
- Bureau of Labor Statistics monthly unemployment reports;
- U.S. Census Wholesale Trade Report;
- U.S. Census Quarterly (New Housing) Sales by Price and Financing;

- U.S. Census Total Construction Spending;
- U.S. Census Retail Trade Report;
- U.S. Census Quarterly Services Survey;
- Commercial Real Estate Survey Credit Reporting Agencies;
- InfoGroup Inc.;
- Business directories; and
- American Community Survey.

While 100% firm coverage is desirable for analysis purposes, the greatest value of BizMiner reports rests in discerning patterns of activity, which are reflected in the large samples used to develop our reports. The overall current coverage of the databases surpasses 13 million active business operations at any point in time.

As is the case with any databases this large, some errors are inevitable. Some firms are missed, and specific information on others is lacking from the database. Not all information received is uniform or complete, resulting in the need to develop projection algorithms for specific industry segments and metrics in some report series. No representation is made as to the accuracy of the databases utilized or the results of subsequent analyses. Neither the Brandow Co. nor its resellers has undertaken independent primary research to confirm the accuracy of the data utilized in the profile analyses. Neither the Brandow Co. nor its resellers are responsible for conclusions drawn or decisions made based upon the data or analysis. In no event will the Brandow Co. or its resellers be liable for any damages, direct, indirect, incidental, or consequential resulting from the use of the information contained in BizMiner reports.

Appendix. Selected Bibliography and Sources of Data

Articles

AICPA, "An Issue Brief on State Marijuana Laws and the CPA Profession," June 18, 2015. www.aicpa.org/advocacy/state/downloadabledocuments/marijuanacpasissuebrief.pdf.

Hilary Bricken, "Top Ten Misconceptions in the Marijuana Industry," Canna Law Blog, Oct. 27, 2014. http://bit.ly/1rWyOU7.

Sam Kamin and Eli Wald, "Marijuana Lawyers: Outlaws or Crusaders?" *Oregon Law Review* (2013), Aug.17, 2012. Available at SSRN: http://bit.ly/1u0BGe0.

Jim Marty, "Ethics Issues for CPAs Working in the Marijuana Industry," *News Account*, Colorado Society of CPAs, March-April 2015, page 16. digital.turn-page.com/i/469978-march-april-2015-newsaccount/3.

Rebecca Millican, "Marijuana and the New Attorney General: Why You Should Care," Canna Law Blog, Oct. 8, 2014. http://bit.ly/1yw1LGZ.

Annette Nellen, "Marijuana and the Tax Law: Issues Faced by Tax Practitioners in Representation of Clients," College of Business at San Jose State University, July 2014. www.sjsu.edu/people/annette.nellen/website/Tax_Ethics_Marijuana_2016.pdf.

Edward J. Roche, "Federal Income Taxation of Medical Marijuana Businesses," Aug. 12, 2013, *Tax Lawyer*, Vol. 66, No. 2, 2013, University of Denver Legal Studies Research Paper No. 13-38. Available at SSRN: http://bit.ly/1EZNqEy.

Karen Ross, "Marijuana, Banking, and the '10-Foot Pole,'" April 28, 2014, Payment Law Advisor. www.paymentlawadvisor.com/2014/04/28/marijuana-banking-and-the-10-foot-pole/.

John Shroyer, "The Famous Marijuana Memos: Q&A With Former DOJ Deputy Attorney General

James Cole," July 27, 2016. mjbizdaily.com/the-famous-marijuana-memos-qa-with-former-doj-deputy-attorney-general-james-cole/.

Regulatory Information

James M. Cole, U.S. Department of Justice, Memorandum, June 29, 2011. www.justice.gov/sites/default/files/oip/legacy/2014/07/23/dag-guidance-2011-for-medical-marijuana-use.pdf.

James M. Cole, U.S. Department of Justice, Memorandum, Aug. 29, 2013. http://1.usa.gov/1da7ofM.

James M. Cole, U.S. Department of Justice, Memorandum, Feb. 14, 2014. www.justice.gov/sites/default/files/usao-wdwa/legacy/2014/02/14/DAG Memo - Guidance Regarding Marijuana Related Financial Crimes 2 14 14 (2).pdf.

W. Thomas McElroy Jr., Office of Chief Counsel, Internal Revenue Service, Memorandum 201504011, Jan. 23, 2015. www.irs.gov/pub/irs-wd/201504011.pdf.

Financial Crimes Enforcement Network, Department of the Treasury, "BSA Expectations Regarding Marijuana-Related Businesses," FIN-2014-G001, Feb. 14, 2014. www.fincen.gov/statutes_regs/guidance/pdf/FIN-2014-G001.pdf.

David W. Ogden, U.S. Department of Justice, Memorandum, Oct. 19, 2009. http://1.usa.gov/11yMHfi.

National Council of State Legislatures, *State Medical Marijuana Laws*, July 20, 2015. http://bit.ly/1udxSs4.

Market and Industry Research Reports

Marijuana Business Factbook 2016
Marijuana Business Media
To purchasers of this report, Marijuana Business Media has graciously provided a $50 discount on the *Marijuana Business Factbook 2016*. To order, please visit MJBizFactbook.com and enter this code: ThanksBVResources50.

Medical & Recreational Marijuana Growing in the US: Market Research Report
Medical & Recreational Marijuana Stores in the US: Market Research Report
IBISWorld Inc.
www.ibisworld.com/industry/medical-recreational-marijuana-growing.html
www.ibisworld.com/industry/medical-recreational-marijuana-stores.html

State of the Emerging Marijuana Industry: Current Trends and Projections
GreenWave Advisors
www.greenwaveadvisors.com

The State of the Legal Marijuana Markets, 4th edition
ArcView Market Research
www.arcviewmarketresearch.com

Trade Associations, Trade Journals, and Blogs

Bridge West CPAs and Consultants
thecannabisindustry.org/tag/bridge-west-llc/

Canna Law Blog
www.cannalawblog.com

Cannabis Business Association
cannabisbusinessassociation.com

Marijuana Business Daily
mjbizdaily.com

Oregon Cannabis Law Group (OCLG) blog
oregonmarijuanalegal.com/oregon-cannabis-law-blog/

www.ingramcontent.com/pod-product-compliance
Ingram Content Group UK Ltd.
Pitfield, Milton Keynes, MK11 3LW, UK
UKHW062006041026
15591UKWH00016B/1191

9 781621 500742